WHO AM I?

A DIFFERENT PERSPECTIVE ON IDENTITY

This book is also available in eBook and French versions.

ISBN: 978-2-95-576568-5
© Published by Pascal Malonda, Paris, 2019
All rights reserved for all countries.

WHO AM I?

A DIFFERENT PERSPECTIVE ON IDENTITY

PASCAL MALONDA

This book is dedicated to you, reader, the one holding this publication in your hands, in the hope that it provides an additional brick to the building representing your identity. Because, as long as the breath of life resides in you, you are destined to grow, to become, and to be.

Pascal Malonda

"For as he thinks within himself, so he is."

(Proverbs 23:7)

Introduction

Nobody can pretend they were like a blank page at birth, for each of us inherits their parents' genetic legacy, which defines their personality traits, and is born in a family with a socio-economic background, which somehow shapes the setting where they are going to take their very first steps. Over the years, experiences, acquaintances, as well as significant events will add to their life story, page after page, thus extending or changing its initial direction. Every story may be personal and unique, but fulfilling it requires the contribution of one or more participants, for it can't write by itself. Everyone's input is different, some being more impactful than others. The fact remains that we should pay careful attention to the people and events we allow in the writing of our life story. Indeed, very few individuals are aware of the effects that society, education system, and entourage can have on one's identity building. To various extents, these multiple actors have nevertheless participated in making who we are today. They have influenced our beliefs, personality, mentality, and way of thinking. Yet, it is very likely that had we lived in another country or culture, some of our deepest convictions would be completely dissimilar. Today, however, they appear as irremovable pillars we built up ourselves upon, on which we lean to exist. The proof is that we tend to believe in what we understand and reject what we don't. We easily accept the principles and reasonings that come our way, as long as they fit in our frame of reference and provided they don't challenge the beliefs we have based our life on. As time goes by, what we incorporate during childhood, adolescence, and adulthood eventually determines the way we perceive things and interact with the world around us.

It is something I experienced in the summer of 2017 while I was on a month's trip in Africa, which gave me the opportunity to visit the Democratic Republic of Congo, Zambia, Malawi, and Mozambique. During the journey, I visited a prison where teenagers were jailed. I was accompanying the members of an association that offers literacy and self-esteem classes. When I saw them, something immediately struck me: their eyes had completely lost the spark and flame that usually characterize the innocence of young boys and ladies with a whole life ahead of them. At first, I thought it was due to captivity and terrible living conditions, but I could sense there was in fact something much deeper. After thinking for a while, I realized this blank look was directly coming from their negative self-image. It was all tarnished by the hardness of their life and the failure cycle driven by jail. It was preventing them from making projections and from believing in a better future. Yet, among them were probably dormant CEOs, teachers, renowned bakers, or who knows, perhaps their country's future president. I was absolutely sure that all the boys had some promising potential, but sadly, they were not granted the necessary and favorable conditions to bloom. Upon leaving them, I was convinced that being in jail wasn't just a matter of deprivation of freedom, but of altered self-perception, too.

Today, how many men and women find themselves in the same situation as these teens? Admittedly, they are physically free, but they also remain prisoners of their own misrepresentation. This raises a fundamental question: **Who am I?**

As long as it stays unanswered, having a true depiction of ourselves is tricky, and so is knowing our authentic life story, for every narrative is articulated around the attributes of its main character. A few years ago, I personally happened to face this self-questioning and it's the reason why the explanations I'm hereby sharing with you are those I found for my own life, as well as by conversing and observing people around me.

With this book, I wish to deliver my vision of identity by taking inspiration from the concepts of three disciplines: sociology, psychology, and faith. Combining these three fields has enabled me to put together a subtler portrayal of Man and his search for identity in a society that promotes national identity, digital identity, sexual identity, but in which human beings keep losing track of who they really are. This misunderstanding results in constant uncertainty within people, thus causing emotional and behavioral disorders, if not depression. Reading this book will lead you to look within yourself, but also to lift up your eyes to the sky, for Man is way too small when confronted with certain existential questions.

This book is divided into two parts:

- The first part "Identity according to Man" describes how society, the education system, entourage, and many other spheres have shaped our system of thought, making us the people we are today.

- The second part "Identity according to God" presents Man as a spiritual being. Although essential for giving a complete and genuine picture of human beings, this point is often ignored.

FIRST PART

Identity according to Man

Chapter 1 – Identity

Located in South America, the Amazon River flows through seven countries: Bolivia, Brazil, Colombia, Ecuador, Guyana, Peru, and Venezuela. Originally it was just a tiny stream flowing down from a mountain, and it went larger and larger over time by accumulating the river waters and other greater rivers along the way. Specialists estimate that over a thousand tributaries flow into the Amazon River, making it one of the largest (6,700 km) and most powerful on Earth (average discharge of 209,000 cubic meters per second)[1], with the Nile. The Amazon River plays a major role throughout the whole region, for it nourishes the Amazon Rainforest and contributes to the life of the entire ecosystem, the fauna and flora. This little stream would have never become the huge river it is today had it not received the supply of multiple water sources. The history of the Amazon River perfectly illustrates what living on Earth is for Man. Born from a simple seed, a child will, year after year, with the participation of numerous internal and external actors, become a teenager, then an adult. Human beings evolve through life by means of the learning process, knowledge, encounters, and experiences. Four seasons compose their life: childhood, adolescence, adulthood/maturity, and old age. Erik Erikson, a famous psychologist, psychoanalyst, and author of

---

1. Wikipedia: https://en.wikipedia.org/wiki/List_of_rivers_by_length

several reference books in behavioral sciences, has developed a theory of psychosocial development that identifies eight stages[2] every healthy individual should pass through.

1-	Infancy (birth to 18 months old). Psychosocial crisis: trust vs. mistrust.	The newborn child is faced with an unfamiliar environment. Adapting to it involves developing a bond of affection with his or her mother and learning to trust her.
2-	Early childhood (18 months to 3 years). Psychosocial crisis: autonomy vs. shame.	Children learn to be self-efficient and take initiative in many activities, including moving around, talking, and eating. Failing from time to time can result in a feeling of embarrassment.
3-	Play age or preschooler (3 to 6 years). Psychosocial crisis: initiative vs. guilt.	Children want to undertake adultlike activities, sometimes overstepping the limits set by their parents. Some actions will put them to the test, and the ones who are unsuccessful may develop feelings of guilt.
4-	School age (7 to 11 years). Psychosocial crisis: industry vs. inferiority.	School encourages children to discover and develop their skills. Inability to complete tasks or unpleasant remarks from adults can create a growing feeling of inferiority. That is why the comments made by adults are so important.
5-	Adolescence (12 to 18-20 years). Psychosocial crisis: identity vs. role confusion.	Adolescents are unsure of their identity, and thus tend to question what they have been taught so far. According to Erikson, they go through an identity crisis.
6-	Young adulthood (20 to 40 years). Psychosocial crisis: intimacy vs. isolation.	Young adults seek companionship and love with others. If unsuccessful, feelings of loneliness or emotional isolation may occur.
7-	Adulthood (40 to 65 years). Psychosocial crisis: generativity vs. stagnation.	Generativity involves contributing to the development of others through counselling and guidance. Those who do not master this task may experience stagnation and withdrawal.
8-	Maturity (65 and older). Psychosocial crisis: integrity vs. despair.	As older adults, some look back with a feeling of integrity and try to make sense out of their lives. They either feel a sense of satisfaction, or rather deal with the end of their lives with despair, if they are overwhelmed with regret.

---

2. Erik Erikson, *"Childhood and society"*, 1950: https://www.simplypsychology.org/Erik-Erikson.html

Each step is described by Erik Erikson as a necessary pillar for entering a new stage of life. In order to best describe the transition from one stage to another, he uses the word <u>crisis</u>, for during this period, two opposing tendencies actually emerge, one being positive and the other negative. For example, the stage called *"intimacy versus isolation"* well illustrates the fact that during that time, individuals face a choice: either build relationships where they run the risk of opening up to develop a strong and durable bond, or remain on the surface, which can lead to isolation, due to superficial relationships. Opposing the two is necessary, for it helps building the ME and therefore one's identity or sense of self[3].

Understanding the changes that occur throughout our life helps us better comprehend how we function. In this chapter, we are going to focus on the different stages of childhood, adolescence, and adulthood, in order to better understand why we talk, think, and behave in one way or another. Thus, we will see how, by using mathematical-like language, **each adult can be seen as the sum of knowledge, ideas, and experiences accumulated over childhood and adolescence.**

- **Childhood**

Transitioning from childhood to adulthood is so natural that we pay little attention to it, while most beliefs, habits, elements of thought and reasoning actually establish at that period of time and will later influence our adult life. Experts estimate that a child's brain develops from zero to five years. During that time, the brain stores a huge amount of information thanks to billions of connections known as *synapses*, between neurons, which generate complex neuronal circuits.

---

3. Erik Erikson, see Wikipedia: https://en.wikipedia.org/wiki/Erik_Erikson

Stephen J. Smith, Professor of Molecular and Cellular Physiology at the Stanford University School of Medicine, said: *"A typical healthy human brain contains about 200 billion nerve cells, or neurons, linked to one another via hundreds of trillions of tiny contacts called synapses.[4]"*. His research has also shown that a single human brain has more switches than all the Internet connections on Earth[5]. Can you possibly understand the complexity of this huge network operating within a small organ that weighs less than 1,500 grams? These connections are fundamental because they allow people to instantly access key pieces of information, once processed several times. As children get older, a massive network expands all over their brain, thereby creating some neuronal architecture that evolves according to their most frequent life experiences. This architecture serves as the basis for personality and thought system development.

Over twenty years ago, I was vacationing on the Caribbean island of Saint Martin, hosted by some relatives. One of my little cousins aged three or four had been watching a rooster eat for a few minutes, which she seemed to find intriguing. At some point, she looked at me and naively asked, like most kids do:

Uncle Pascal, what is it?

- *"It's a rooster", I said.*
- *What is the rooster eating?*

---

4. Interview of Stephen Smith. See article: *"New imaging method developed at Stanford reveals stunning details of brain connection"*, published by the Stanford Medicine University on November 17, 2010: https://med.stanford.edu/news/all-news/2010/11/new-imaging-method-developed-at-stanford-reveals-stunning-details-of-brain-connections.html
5. See also: https://www.cnet.com/news/human-brain-has-more-switches-than-all-computers-on-earth/

- *It's eating seeds.*
- *Why is it eating seeds?*
- *In order to feed itself.*
- *Who is the rooster's wife?*
- *It's the hen.*
- *But where does the hen come from?*
- *The hen comes from the egg.*
- *And where does the egg come from?*
- *...*

At that moment, I have to admit that I gave up and ended our talk, being totally unable to answer her question, point of origin of a debate as old as the hills, which she couldn't know. Yet, she was just being ordinarily curious, as kids in the middle of the experimental phase can be. Each question would enable her to broaden her knowledge by matching what she could see with what it actually represented. Following every answer of mine, her brain would perform some invisible work. This principle applies to positive as well as negative things. A friend once told me that as he was at the table with his wife and their four-year-old son, his little boy used a bad word in mid-conversation. It was so crude that it caused a moment of silence. My friend calmly asked him: *"Where did you hear this?"*, and his son named one of his schoolmates. The latter had probably heard an adult pronounce the bad word and had memorized it. The dad looked at his wife and said: *"We have to leave this town!"* He was worried because of the neighborhood and the school's ability to teach bad values to his child. The following year, they executed their project and moved to a nicer town with a better school environment.

Brain is not static, it unceasingly evolves over time, especially when it comes to learning and memorization phases, during which it creates or develops its structure by reorganizing its nervous system. Neuroscience calls this ability neuroplasticity, or brain plasticity. An official issue published by the OECD (Organization for Economic Co-operation and Development) quoted the results of recent brain studies in which the discoveries made by neuroscientists on this subject are explained: "*Neuroscientists clearly demonstrated that our brain can considerably adapt to the requirements of its environment, also known as plasticity, in science. Some neural connections are made and strengthened, while others are weakened or eliminated, depending on the brain's needs.[6]*". Individuals who learn new things on a regular basis and who constantly evolve force their brain to continuously create and modify new neural connections, unlike the ones who do not change their habits, do not evolve, and remain stuck with the same way of thinking and reasoning. The former regularly build, modify, reshape their neural network, whereas the latter keep it still, rigid, and static. Consequently, no external transformation can occur unless internal changes happen first. Already heard this, haven't you? Neuroscience evidences today that the changes occurring in the brain are not just mental, but also cerebral, therefore structural.

A friend told me that during their first year of marriage, he and his wife had to change their way of doing things on many fronts, one of them being the dishes. As funny as it may sound, he explained that once he'd be done eating, he would always wash his plate and cutlery right away, while his wife would leave them on the counter or in the sink, sometimes for

---

6. Issue published under the responsibility of the OECD General Secretary: "*Comprendre le cerveau: naissance d'une science de l'apprentissage*", 2007, p.13

days. They both had inherited these habits from their parents. Needless to say, some tensions arose in the beginning. He quickly understood that the real issue was not about knowing who was right or wrong, given they each had the impression that their behavior was normal, having become their own personal habit. They eventually adjusted their respective ways of thinking in order to find how to work things out as a couple. An inner change within themselves had to occur first, so that it would become externally visible thereafter.

In that respect, it is essential to learn, listen, watch, and experience good things while being young, because it enables one to build healthy foundations which will help them become adults in good physical, emotional, and spiritual health. In this regard, Doctor Caroline Leaf wrote: *As a matter of fact, each memory is connected to a matching emotion that is stored in your brain, comparable to a photocopy in your body cells*[7]. On the other hand, any traumatizing experience, negative event, or belittling word can leave deep inner wounds which, if not healed early enough, may wreck internally to the point where it can alter one's life path.

Several childhood and adolescence studies have revealed that children who enjoy a nurturing environment, favorable for their development and well-being, where they are loved, listened to, and educated with compassion are much more likely to become fulfilled and successful adults. In the opposite case, children suffering from self-esteem issues, severe shyness, or inferiority complex have certainly lacked consideration and encouraging words from their peers. As adults, they will face difficulties when joining a group, building social and professional relationships, and overall, they may struggle to have a happy and fulfilling life. Caused by physical or psychological

---

7. Caroline Leaf: *"Who switched off my brain?"*, p.21

abuse, emotional wounds can generate a continuous failure cycle, if not prevented. An articled published in Psychology Today explains the possible outcomes of this in an adult's life:

Children make meaning out of the events they witness and the things that happen to them, and they create an internal map of how the world is. This meaning-making helps them cope. But if children don't create a new internal map as they grow up, their old way of interpreting the world can damage their ability to function as adults[8].

Just as house construction requires solid foundations to ensure stability, childhood and adolescence are key periods which contribute to one's evolution and personality development.

- **Adolescence**

Psychologist James E. Marcia further developed Erik Erikson's research by dividing adolescence into four parts[9] (1996). During that stage, adolescents are faced with a gamut of situations that will force them to voice their own choices, and the approach they pick plays a part in structuring their identity. For many parents, adolescence rhymes with going through major upheavals, for during that time not only do they feel they don't know their child anymore, but communication often becomes a huge issue. The teenage years mark the transition from childhood to adulthood, forcing adolescents to ask

---

8. Andrea Brandt : "*4 Ways the Pain of Childhood Trauma Impacts Us as Adults*", article published by Psychology Today on June 01, 2017: https://www.psychologytoday.com/blog/mindful-anger/201706/4-ways-the-pain-childhood-trauma-impacts-us-adults
9. James E. Marcia, the four identity statuses of psychological identity development: foreclosure, identity diffusion, moratorium, and identity achievement. Wikipedia: https://en.wikipedia.org/wiki/James_Marcia

themselves who they really are and what they want to become. As they get older, they will increasingly assert their identity, and they will be challenged by all sorts of questions and situations requiring them to make choices, and sometimes to take a stand. Moreover, they permanently seek answers from their schoolmates, or through the conversations they have with their friends belonging to the same social groups (sports, music, art, etc.), the same location (neighborhood, city, ...), and also by learning from the successful ones, seen as role models among the community. They have to choose between do's and don'ts, good and bad, the principles taught by their parents and those of their friends, sometimes totally opposite. At that age, teenagers tend to compare themselves to others, and their self-perception depends on how others see them. The ones with a pretty weak personality are likely to follow the majority in order to please and to be accepted, because their priority is what others think about them. Driven by their quest for identity, many adolescents picture their heroes and favorite celebrities as mentors, to the point where they will dress like them, copy their hairstyles, and imitate both their vocabulary and behavior.

I live near a high school and watching this mirroring phenomenon is quite entertaining. A few years ago, I was amused to see some teenage girls with "half hawk" haircuts, that is long hair on one side and shaved hair on the other half. These girls were in fact influenced by their favorite stars, such as Miley Cyrus, Rihanna, and Avril Lavigne. Nothing new under the sun, you might say, considering many of us did the same thing at that age.

For some, being 13-14 is synonymous with first cigarettes, introduction to alcohol, as well as first risky sexual experiences, despite all the possible prevention and educational programs as a response to the many dangers associated. Most of the time, it's all about contesting parental authority, or feeling like an adult, or simply doing the same things as everyone in order to feel accepted in a group. Turning 16 or 17 marks self-affirmation and represents the last steps before reaching the age of majority, namely freedom. However, this newly acquired independence should be carefully used, for if some individuals are reasonable enough to turn corners with caution, others jump head-first into their new life before realizing it can morph into a prison, if improperly used. Several surveys show that this journey of assertiveness and self-discovery comes with a period of risk, as evidenced by the results of a study conducted by MAIF Insurance[10]:

- From 14 to 18 years old, one in three deaths is caused by a car accident.

- In fatal crashes, 30% are alcohol-related and 10% cannabis-related: mixing the two increases risks.

- 40% of teenagers aged 15, and 57% aged 17 report having ever been drunk.

- 30% of teenagers aged between 13 and 15 report having ever smoked cannabis, one in five being a regular smoker.

On top of that, depression is, according to a report published by WHO, *"the predominant cause of illness and disability for both boys and girls aged 10 to 19 years.*[11]*"* During that time, double transformation takes place, given it

---

10. Maif Insurance website, see document: *"L'adolescence et les conduites à risques"*: https://www.maif.fr/content/pdf/la-maif-s-engage/actions-mutualistes/adolescence-et-conduites-a-risques/maif-essentiel-sur-adolescent-et-conduites-a-risque.pdf
11. World Health Organization, *"WHO calls for stronger focus on adolescent health"*, May 14, 2014: http://www.who.int/mediacentre/news/releases/2014/focus-adolescent-health/en/

operates biologically, with puberty and the accompanying body changes, and psychologically, with confusing changing perceptions and understanding of the world. Adolescence enables young people to say goodbye to childhood and become more or less fulfilled adults, depending on the way they experienced their teenage years. Psychologist Stanley Hall uses strong words, since he even talks about a **new birth**. He says: *"Adolescence is a new birth, for the higher and more completely human traits are now born[12]"*.

- **Adulthood**

Looking at the various stages of personal development allows us to realize how, from childhood to adulthood, we are not always aware of the journey we are going through, moving from one phase to another. Like a stair climb, each step prepares us to the next level, until we finally reach adulthood. Adulthood is not an end in itself because obviously we keep evolving, but on the basis of the foundations built over childhood and adolescence. Understanding this helps us better grasp that the way we talk, think, and act as adults is not trivial at all, but totally aligned with how our inner self was continuously transformed.

The environment we live and evolve in is fundamental, for that framework actually shapes our inner self by influencing how we think and behave. Every life season is important; however, scientists agree that childhood and adolescence play an even more crucial role, in laying the groundwork for personality and identity building. The Larousse dictionary defines identity as: *"the permanent and fundamental characteristics*

---

12. Brainy Quote website, see: https://www.brainyquote.com/quotes/g_stanley_hall_381305?src=t_teen

of a person or a group, de facto characterizing their individuality and peculiarity". In psychology, philosophy, and sociology, the concept of identity often varies, depending on tiny nuances. But if we had to gather and merge them all into one single definition, we could simply say: **identity is an individual's self-awareness**. Admittedly, this lifelong process rests on the various phases we explore, and the maturity we gain from each. The way we perceive ourselves is personal because it is based on the criteria we have internalized, which now act as filters through which we see the world, but also ourselves. Author Cameron C. Taylor wrote: *"People do not see the world as it is, they see it as they are*[13]*"*.

---

13. Cameron C. Taylor, *"8 Attributes of great achievers"*, Ed. Embassy Books, p.103

Summary:

- A human's life has four seasons: childhood, adolescence, maturity, and old age.

- Experts believe that a child's brain undergoes an amazing period of development from zero to five years. As children get older, a huge network grows in the brain, memorizing a large amount of information.

- Although each season of life is important, specialists agree that childhood and adolescence play a crucial role because they lay the groundwork for personality and identity building.

- Identity is a person's self-awareness, it is the image they see in the mirror of their soul.

Questions:

- What image do you have of yourself? Is it good or bad? Explain why accordingly.

- If you had to define yourself, what would you say?

- Which bad habits and behaviors acquired during childhood would you like to change or quit today?

- During childhood and adolescence, what have you done or said in order to please and to be accepted by your friends which you now regret?

- Do you have childhood wounds still affecting you today in your adult life? If so, what are they?

Chapter 2 – The thought process

About 10 years ago, I was on a plane off to Lisbon, Portugal, with my friend Jean-Marc. We were to join a group of friends renting a house there. Due to the peak summer season and because we had booked last-minute tickets, we had to stop in Zurich, Switzerland, for a layover. Fifty minutes after take-off, the pilot made an in-flight announcement about imminent turbulence, and asked us to fasten our seat belts. Immediately after, the aircraft started to shake violently with vibrating wings, and the ride went bumpier and bumpier, some air pockets giving the impression that the plane was literally dropping several meters. Panic spread among the passengers, the jolts being so impressive that everybody could tell it was not just the usual moderate turbulence frequent travelers are used to. As the plane was still bouncing in all directions, I suddenly remembered that a year earlier, an aircraft of the same airline had tragically crashed in Germany. I then started an inner dialogue with myself. *"Do you realize that about a year ago, a plane from the exact same company crashed down! We always think it only happens to others, but maybe the passengers aboard the other plane were thinking the same, and yet it did happen to them!"* While I was immersed in my thoughts, my monologue was interrupted by another endless drop and by some screams coming from the back of the plane. I turned around and was unpleasantly surprised to see a flight attendant. Totally distressed, she let herself sink into her seat, fastened her seat belt, and gripped her armrest. "*That's all we needed!*", I told myself. Fear invaded the rest of the cabin. I looked around me, nobody was chatting anymore. Everybody was having an internal dialogue with themselves. What could they be telling themselves? Some were certainly praying their respective gods, while others were thinking of their loved ones, or seeing their life flash before their eyes. As for me, I was talking to God. Although I had deserted the church benches years ago and I would only pray on special occasions, I really felt that at that very moment, being up in the air between sky and earth, He was the only one who could help. My prayers weren't based on a constant relationship I had with Him, but rather on the childhood memories I was clinging to, which helped me to rely on faith at that precise moment. Between two sharp drops, I begged God: "*Please, do something! Please, do something! If I survive, I'll do this and that...*" I then listed a series of good resolutions I would probably not remember once hitting the ground again. My friend Jean-Marc later admitted that despite his calm appearance, he had been praying too. Turbulence eventually vanished and slowly gave way to a relaxing atmosphere. Livid faces got their color back and people started to chat again. Silence didn't actually mean they had stopped talking, but their dialogue had simply become internal. As long as a person is alive, they can't stop thinking, and they just carefully choose what they want to voice out loud. Right after landing, we warmly applauded the pilots, and I thanked God for hearing my prayers.

I didn't get a chance to gather the other passengers' impressions, but I know, after seeing their faces, that nobody experienced the hectic flight the same way. All you had to do was watch their body language and behavior. Some were totally stoic, others anxious or freaked out. Given the circumstances, everyone's reactions were totally understandable. The wind had been shaking the aircraft up and down and left to right as if it was a meaningless puppet, not to mention the creaking wings, the loud engine, and the jaw-dropping sudden plunges. There is another key point I would like to emphasize, something way less noticeable but extremely important, because it undoubtedly influenced one another's reactions. Indeed, this element processed all the information sent to the brain through the five senses, before transferring it to the body via emotions. For example, the eyes witnessed the wings fighting against the wind, and people's petrified faces. The ears heard the creaking wings, the loud engine, and the panicked screams. Some passengers' hands probably went sweaty and forcefully grasped the seats to prevent their bodies from being shaken back and forth. People were likely to have dry mouths, noses, and throats, besides breathing heavily due to both stress and air conditioning. The numerous pieces of information and sensations were interpreted differently, depending on the passengers' profile. I will now show you what possibly happened in everyone's head, so you understand the central role of **thoughts**.

In order to make it easier, let's split the passengers into 3 groups:

- One, those who fear flying.

- Two, those who do not fear flying.

- Three, the ones who were not scared during the flight.

These groups aim to help better understand why they all reacted in a different way, depending on their personality, temper, and personal background. It is important to underline that **every spoken word, emotion, or action of ours**

emanates from a subtle mechanism. In the first place, a thought or feeling is expressed, then analyzed and custom-reshaped if necessary, so that it matches our internal parameters, such as personality, sensitivity, mentality, knowledge, and intelligence. This process doesn't only apply to special circumstances, but occurs every time we have to act, speak, or perform a task of any kind.

The scheme below shows how this mechanism operates and is repeated upon every action, spoken word, or emotion:

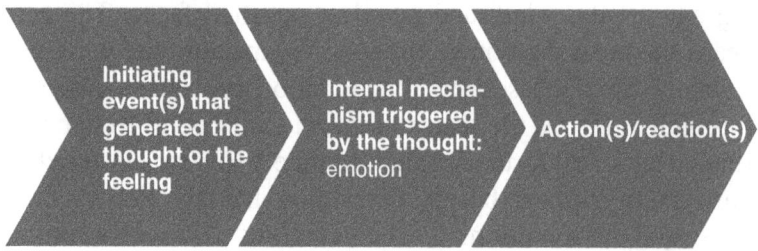

- **Group 1: passengers who fear flying**

As for those, it's easy to imagine how difficult overcoming this situation must have been. There might be various reasons behind their fear of flying. We can suppose some simply dislike the sensation of height or of void. Others are probably completely terrified of death, which encourages them to imagine the worst when they end up thousands of feet above the ground, and especially after hearing all the tragic plane crash stories reported by the media. These are just two examples helping us to better comprehend how the people of this category were already doomed to fear flying. There is every reason to think that immediately after the first jolt, their hearts were racing, and they were paralyzed by fear and anxiety.

| Predisposition to fear of flying: feeling of unease and stress | Emotions triggered by the thoughts: fear, panic, anxiety | Reactions: increased heart rate, sweaty hands, grabbing onto the seats |

- **Group 2: passengers who do not fear flying**

This group concerns those who, like Jean-Marc and I, generally don't fear flying. However, considering the exceptional nature of the situation, fear eventually dominated us. We did not undergo this event like the ones of Group 1, because anxiety hit us much later. We are not afraid of flying, we don't have any fear of heights, nor do we have any negative memories of flights that ended badly. When everything happened, we paid no attention at the beginning, partly because too excited about our vacation. Yet, when the bumps gained intensity and the situation worsened, doubts invaded our thoughts and brought fear then terror along the way. Fear peaked when we heard the flight attendant scream. Like the first group, we were in turn haunted by panic, but although the mechanism remains the same, the way of interpreting events is far different.

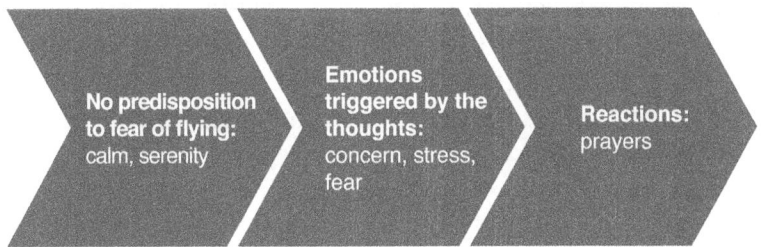

| No predisposition to fear of flying: calm, serenity | Emotions triggered by the thoughts: concern, stress, fear | Reactions: prayers |

- **Group 3: passengers who were not scared during the flight**

As for the third group, it comprises those who were not scared during the entire flight. I doubt there were many. According to you, who could they be? Believers, confident God would save them from imminent death? The pilots? Soldiers? Parachutists? Bold ones? We happened to notice that as experienced and prepared as she was, the flight attendant herself lost it pretty quickly. Whoever these people are, profiling them briefly helps us understand how they managed to stay calm, compared to the rest: they were just thinking differently.

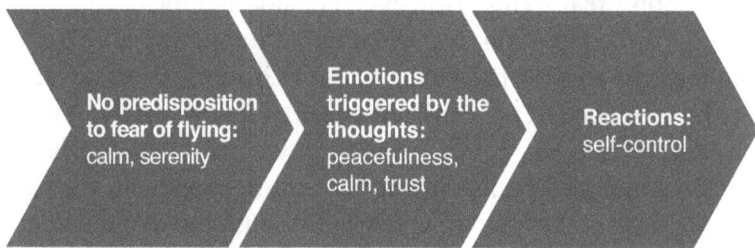

Classifying the passengers into three groups clearly highlights the fact that although they faced the same critical situation, one another's reactions were totally unalike, depending on how they looked at things. Each person interpreted what they went through in accordance with their way of thinking. **The thoughts generated by an individual plainly define who they are, what they understand, and why they tend to react in one way or another**. The way a person thinks is no coincidence: it stems from a thorough process, as just discussed.

- **The thought process**

    So, what is it exactly? **The thought process is the mechanism which enables one to interpret and interact with the world, using the mindsets they have continuously developed throughout their life.** Every individual is unique, and so are their personal background and way of thinking. **Speech is the outer world's language, while thoughts are that of the inner world.** They refer to the ideas, reflections, and images shaped or received within oneself. Those are fueled by people themselves, through their concerns, conversations, aspirations, emotions, and frustrations collected in their environment. Over the centuries, several conflicting schools of thought have emerged, debating over how human thoughts are created in the first place. Even today, their points of disagreement remain, and they are far from having reached consensus. There are:

    Those who believe that human beings are simply made up of matter, and see thoughts as the result of physical brain activity, only. Among them is Patricia Churchland, an American neurophilosopher, who wrote:

    "Bit by experimental bit, neuroscience is morphing our conception of what we are. The weight of evidence now implies that it is the brain, rather than some nonphysical stuff, that feels, thinks, and decides. That means there is no soul to fall in love. We do still fall in love, certainly, and passion is as real as it ever was. The difference is that now we understand those important feelings to be events happening in the physical brain. It means that there is no soul to spend its postmortem eternity blissful in Heaven or miserable in Hell[1]".

---

1. Patricia Churchland, *"Brain-wise: Studies in Neurophilosophy"*, 2002, p.1

Those believing that humans beings are much more than just atoms perceive thoughts as the soul's internal dialogue.

- **Our thought process**

Human beings can display several "public" faces, depending on the current context or the people around them, but on the other hand, they have just one single intimate private face which they only reveal to a small circle of people, if anyone. This "intimate" facet is the closest one to who we really are, without artifice or false pretenses, nor setup to fit in with other people. Our attitude and behavior are just a tiny bit of exhibition of what's constantly taking place in our mind, for we never cease to think all day long. They are the true reflections of our inner selves, or, for those essentially driven by emotions, of their strong personality traits, addictions, and even what controls them. Our thoughts play a crucial role in our everyday life, for we produce an average of 30,000 to 50,000 thoughts a day. The dominating thoughts repeatedly generated every day end up becoming an integral part of ourselves, thus shaping our personality.

Summary:

- The thoughts we produce eventually determine who we are, what we understand, and why we react in one way or another.

- Speech is the outer world's language, while thoughts are that of the inner world.

- The thought process is the mechanism which enables one to interpret and interact with the world, using the mindsets they have continuously developed throughout their life.

- Numerous scientists and philosophers consider that Man is just a product of evolution, whereas others assume Man derives from Creation. The former believe that Man is his brain, whereas the latter argue that he is endowed with a spirit and/or a soul.

Questions:

- What kind of thoughts do you have daily? Are they rather positive or negative? If you tend to have negative thoughts, can you write them down and explain the reasons behind them?

- When realizing how your thoughts and emotions can impact your life, what would you like to readjust in order to become a better person?

- The plane testimony demonstrates how powerful thoughts and emotions are. Do you control your thoughts and emotions, or are you dominated by them instead?

Chapter 3 – Personality

We reached seven billion inhabitants in the world in 2011, every single one of us standing out thanks to their biological characteristics and personality. An article published on the BBC website in January 2017 revealed seven ways of identifying a person from the rest of the world, as unique[1]. These seven features are: the shape of their ears, their body odor, the way they walk, their backside, skull, fingernails, and the pores on their nose. Aren't you amazed that out of seven billion people, such tiny details are specific to each individual? This peculiarity isn't just physical. It also concerns everyone's personality, composed of a brilliant blend of stories, encounters, and experiences. It comprises both what's innate and what's acquired over time, hence the complexity. Innate refers to the genes, the personality traits inherited from one's parents, whereas acquired in the result of family upbringing, educational background, culture, influence of friends and colleagues, as well as many other factors. Multiple actors get involved at various stages of our life, each being more or less important, but I would like to focus on four of them, responsible for building the foundations many of our convictions rest

---

1. BBC, *"The seven ways you are totally unique"*, article published on January 10, 2017: http://www.bbc.com/future/story/20170109-the-seven-ways-you-are-totally-unique

on, together with our knowledge and habits. Those are **family, education, society, and the media**. By closely looking at them, you will see that our convictions are not random at all: on the contrary, most have been transmitted and taught to us, or are the consequences of our environment's influence and cultural heritage.

1 - Family

In 1988, French singer Maxime Le Forestier wrote a song entitled "Né quelque part", which translates as "born somewhere". The song starts with a simple and filled with truth sentence: "We don't choose our parents, we don't choose our family". No newborn is in control of the place they're born in, nor the one they will be raised in. They suddenly open their eyes some day and find themselves face to face with the one who carried them in the womb for nine months. If birth symbolizes happiness for most parents, it sometimes triggers the exact opposite for others, who will opt to abandon the unwanted child or who just can't take care of him or her. The living conditions a child evolves and becomes an adult in differ a lot from one family, country, and culture, to another. The parents' role is pivotal because they are the ones in charge of creating the family atmosphere, which is not a matter of comfort or financial resources (although wealth can be synonymous with quality of life), but rather of love, joy, attention, unity, and the values in place. Some children are lucky enough to grow up in a loving and caring household, which obviously nurtures their well-being and personal development. Others, on the other hand, suffer from verbal and/or physical abuse, as well as indifference. Sometimes, indifference negatively impacts someone's life as much as verbal, even physical abuse.

The family environment plays a crucial role in children's development, for it represents the place where they build and shape their identity in receiving their parents' education, values, principles, beliefs, traditions, and culture. Generally, parents also endeavor to teach the society's rules, values, and norms so that, by incorporating and respecting them, children live harmoniously with their peers. Additionally, the parents' role in child development is key because both set an example at an age when children look for reference models. Indeed, children tend to imitate spontaneously what they see, their parents being the first inspirational examples—good or bad—they will learn from to project themselves into the future. The way they talk, live, and behave represents countless data stored somewhere in the child's brain, used to help them understand the world around them and better analyze the transmitted information.

Doctor Rick Rigsby delivered an empowering speech over a graduation ceremony. During the lecture, he explained how his degree-less father was a role model for him and his brother, through his lifestyle, principles, work, and discipline. His father passed on his core values to them, and applying those in their everyday life enabled them to succeed and have brilliant career paths. In his passionate speech, he said: "*I have four degrees. My brother is a judge. We're not the smartest ones in our family. It's a third-grade dropout daddy²*". Rick Rigsby acknowledged that his father's value didn't reside in degrees, but in being the inspirational model he always was.

---

2. Rick Rigsby, "Lessons from a third-grade dropout" speech. Youtube link: https://www.youtube.com/watch?v=Bg_Q7KYWG1g

- **The impact of family dysfunctions**

    When the role of the home environment isn't fully fulfilled, children are the first victims. Today, specialists have to deal with 13-year-old repeat offenders or underage girls voluntarily prostituting themselves for money. Some are placed and treated in special youth centers, in the hope that a change of environment impacts them positively. But after some time, some run away, and start all over again. Their behavior only being the tip of the iceberg, diving into the submerged part is necessary in order to analyze the background, history, and events that led them to such misconduct. As a matter of fact, in such cases, the only efficient way to put things right is to focus efforts on understanding what provoked the bad actions in the first place, rather than the effects or symptoms themselves. Indeed, the latter are just a consequence, therefore treating them wouldn't completely work because the root cause of the problem has to be fixed first. A report published by the Ministry of Justice in 2013 provides statistics on juvenile delinquency in France:

    In 2013, there were an estimated 14.6 million minors under 18 in France. That year, 234,000 of them were involved in criminal cases. 9% were aged under 13, 40% between 13 and 15, and 47% were 16 or 17. 83% of them were boys.

    The report underlines that several factors need to be taken into account for a proper understanding of the reasons, including: *"academic failure, socio-economic issues, housing in neighborhoods of relegation, as well as the parental relationship quality and parental vigilance*[3]*"*.

---

3. Ministry of Justice report, *"La délinquance des mineurs"*, published in 2013: http://www.justice.gouv.fr/publication/o45_resume_2.pdf

- **The importance of love**

While it is true that no family is perfect, home still remains the best place for a human being, when it comes to receiving love and learning to love in return, which allows men and women to become at ease with themselves. A person's emotional balance often depends on the attention and love they get from their family. An adult who received enough love during childhood is likewise capable of giving some to others, who in turn become bearers of love. **There is nothing more powerful on Earth than love, and every human being desperately needs love to feel alive.** Just imagine a flower without sun. Over time, it would dry out, lose its glow and beauty, and die. The same goes for men and women who don't receive enough love. The same way a thirsty soil cries after the rain, Man's heart is hungry of love. According to you, what would happen in a suddenly loveless society? It would only be a short matter of time before it becomes completely unlivable. There would be no values, no respect, no solidarity. No civilization can cope with such rough climate, for absence of love means hate, and hate is the greatest evil. Nowadays, the word love has lost its full meaning because it refers to physical and romantic relationships in many people's minds, while it has a much larger scope that touches all spheres of life. The French language has only one single word for love: *amour*, while there are two in English: *love* and *like*, and four in Ancient Greek. In English, *love* generally involves deep feelings, whereas *like* is more of a tender feeling toward someone, or simply something one enjoys. In Ancient Greek, the four distinct words for *love* are much more meaningful because they clearly make a distinction between the levels and particularities of love. *"Phileo"* represents tender affection or friendship, *"Storgê"* is the love you share with your family, *"Éros"* refers to passionate love and physical attraction, and *"Agapè"* means unconditional love.

The pedestal of a nation doesn't just rest on respecting its laws, principles, and values, as we tend to think. For coexistence to be possible and especially pleasant, each citizen should at least love themselves first before they can love others. Otherwise, social cohesion can't survive. Remove love, and you'll see that after a while, laws and values no longer have any power. **When the police are in charge of maintaining public order, family, for its part, is in charge of maintaining love within a nation.** This approach can sound utopian because it is neither tangible nor measurable, but a country's good condition first depends on the good condition of its families.

2 - Teaching

All political leaders willing to see their country develop, prosper, and shine on the international scene choose to invest in education, for it enables to train and prepare the men and women of tomorrow's society. The governments of developed countries tend to assign a significant share of their national budget to education, considering it one of the central pillars of a nation and of its public policy. Instruction having such power, as history shows, some leaders have felt free to exploit it for personal purposes. This is how some authoritarian regimes, intending to maintain the stranglehold on their country by controlling the populations, changed the school curriculums to their advantage by praising their ideas and congratulating themselves. The school was then used as a propaganda tool in order to root their ideologies in the minds of the youth, thus ensuring the durability of their reign by formatting the people's way of thinking. By doing this, once the children would become adults, they would remain under control, having inevitably absorbed the authoritarian ideas. It is exactly what happened in Germany with the creation of the Hitler Youth. Hitler established an organization aiming to physically and militarily train young boys aged six to eighteen and teach them the Nazi theories. Indoctrinating them intended to brainwash the youngest generations with the Nazi ideology, to keep them under control, and manipulate them as they pleased. The organization had reached over five million in 1936[4]. The same happened with Benito Mussolini, who used the Italian education system to spread his ideology. Here is an extract from a history book on the subject:

"Mussolini, whose mother was a teacher and who had been a teacher, too, quickly understood that school and especially primary school was, in an Italy hit by high rates of illiteracy, the only institution to be possibly regarded as the "People's School", therefore the perfect place to indoctrinate children and teenagers. The utmost importance was thereby attached to primary school books, predominantly, to the extent that they were the only manuals with effective obligation, planned and prepared accordingly under the command of ministers and hierarchs of the National Fascist Party[5]".

These examples evidence how the instruction and education received by young individuals ultimately determine their future selves, as adults. It is no coincidence that dictators exploit the school systems as propaganda tools to spread their ideas, for as mentioned earlier, childhood and adolescence are key stages in one's identity building. We could think these techniques belong to the past, but countries like North Korea demonstrate that unfortunately, these practices still exist nowadays. An article published in Opinion Internationale in 2014 describes how the North Korean school system works: *"North*

---

4. Wikipedia: https://en.wikipedia.org/wiki/Hitler_Youth
5. Mariella Colin, *"Les livres de lecture italiens pour l'école primaire sous le fascisme (1923-1943)"*, p.57
See: https://histoire-education.revues.org/2243

Korea's government doesn't seek to stimulate the children's brains and autonomy. It simply aims to build docile clones that will obey the regime. Education only exists to teach them how to blindly serve the Kim dynasty's policy, and thus avoid any possible uprising[6]." The North Korean government wants to keep its citizens servile and docile by restricting access to knowledge, in order to keep controlling them. If the state takes such precautions, it is because access to knowledge can encourage people to launch a revolution and overthrow the current government.

- **Instruction or education**

Education focuses on developing social skills and manners by adhering to a given culture, its social codes, rules, and moral values. The word education originates from the Latin *educatio*, derived from the verb *educere*, which means to lead out, to guide. The Académie Française (French Academy) defines education as giving children and teenagers all the necessary attention for developing their physical, intellectual, and moral capacities[7]. This responsibility first rests with the child's parents, then with the schooling system. Instruction, on the other hand, consists in passing on knowledge to someone. Instruct comes from the Latin verb *instruere*, meaning to construct, to build. Instruction makes it possible to *build* someone from the inside by transmitting the knowledge they need. The difference between education and instruction is often debated, especially when it comes to discussing the boundaries of the role of school. It is interesting to remember that before 1832,

---

6. Guillaume Autere, *"Confession d'une jeune Nord-Coréenne"*, article published by Opinion Internationale on November 20, 2014: https://www.opinion-internationale.com/2014/11/20/confessions-dune-jeune-nord-coreenne_31084.html
7. Definition edited by the Académie Française in 1986, see: http://www.la-definition.fr/definition/eduquer

the French national education was called "public instruction", and from that date, it was renamed "*national education*". If the first denomination was more in line with the said mission, historians nevertheless agree that its role was not just limited to instructing, but also educating[8]. The school's field of action has nonetheless expanded in recent years, particularly with the many social issues it had to take up.

- **Schools**

    Once created, the public and republican education sought to emancipate children from the catholic thought. Its original purpose was to pass on and apply, as quoted: "the republican values, secularism, citizenship, culture of commitment, and fight against any form of discrimination". The aspiration of the state is to have informed, educated, free to think, and able to judge for themselves citizens, for knowledge sets people free, and schools tend to apply this principle. Therefore, the first purpose of schools is to establish healthy and strong foundations on which children, teenagers, and adults will rest and build their own opinions and way of thinking.

    However, the boundaries set by the National Education became more and more blurred when it had to deal with issues questioning the parents' education itself. Indeed, many educational institutions are now facing significant problems, formerly reserved to education within the same family, such as: alcoholism, uncontrolled sexuality due to pornography, violence. With the growing lack of communication in families, the education system was forced to address these issues, considered taboo in certain households. That is how schools

---

8. Claude Lelièvre, *"Un ministère d'abord de 'l'Instruction publique'? Et un ministre à l'Éducation Nationale?"*, published by Mediapart on August 25, 2014

happened to educate on a wider array of topics, sometimes being the only interlocutors. If the initial idea is valuable, it is yet extremely important to make sure that schools do not become the "multipurpose tools". This trend is well described in an article written by research officer Olivier Rey, published in some teaching manuals:

"Even so, every time society faces a crisis, we tend to state that the education system is the answer, even before having precisely defined the question. And we multiply the "educations about" in school curriculums, those educations being fueled by actions or remaining perfectly laudable and generous intention-wise, but made outside the school or at its margins in order to inundate the educational actors with kits, devices, guides, and briefcases on such or such touchy issue. In doing so, we are prone to quickly forgetting that teaching is a real job, and supporting a cause is not enough to dispose of the necessary skills needed to train and educate young individuals.[9]"

3 - Society

Very early, parents and education system teach children how to comply with society's rules and principles, for them to fit in and live as part of a community. The reluctant ones are soon excluded and cannot fit in, unless they eventually accept the codes. Therefore, citizens are responsible for adapting to the system, not the contrary, for the weight is such that even mavericks have to at least accept a few points if they want to be able to live and work within the said society. Sociologists call this concept socialization, namely the process through

---

9. Olivier Rey, *"L'école face aux crises de société"*: http://www.cahiers-pedagogiques.com/L-ecole-face-aux-crises-de-societe

which society passes on the culture, values, and social norms to a person, giving them the ability to live, optimally interact with their environment, and build their own identity. Sociologists differentiate between two types of socialization: primary and secondary. **Primary socialization** takes place during childhood and adolescence, when a child's personality and identity formation occurs. **Secondary socialization**, on the other hand, starts in a person's late teens, and continues for the rest of their life. In the primary socialization phase, the influential actors are mainly family, school, and friends, while in the secondary socialization phase, they are rather colleagues, acquaintances, and some people met within varying social groups such as church, cultural, and sports activities[10].

- **The power of influence**

The word influence is used all over the place today, whether in leadership, psychology, personal development, or in the media, some even going so far as to say that we are living in the age of influence. Influence refers to the capacity to guide the opinion of someone or of a group, in a particular direction. For example, it can mean to follow and adopt the ideas of someone we admire because they stand out thanks to their spirit, talent, intelligence, or success. To further illustrate this point, let's take the example of the social media "influencers". Nowadays, many more or less famous celebrities are called influencers, just because the content they post on social networks is followed by enough people to become new trends, out of nothing. It is a new phenomenon since before these networks, a so-called influencer was in fact someone who had achieved major accomplishments or left their mark on

---

10. La Toupie website, see: http://www.toupie.org/Dictionnaire/Socialisation_primaire_secondaire.htm

future generations (e.g. politicians, artists, inventors, doctors, researchers, astronauts, etc.). Now, one can become an influencer out of thin air... The power of influence can be beneficial when the author conveys a positive message which helps others become better persons, just like it can be negative when the message is pernicious. That is how, with their accomplishments, some men and women have influenced generations, and they keep doing so even long after their passing.

- **The influence of culture**

Understanding another country is challenging for a foreigner, especially when not familiar with its people's culture. UNESCO[11] commonly defines culture as: *"that complex whole which includes knowledge, beliefs, arts, morals, laws, customs, and any other capabilities and habits acquired by a human as a member of society."*[12] Sometimes, the citizens who make up a nation originate from very diverse geographic, cultural, and social lands, but what unites one another is the cultural identity they have in common. For that reason, **culture is regarded as the people's identity.**

- **The influence of the social environment**

In his book entitled "The spirit of leadership", writer Myles Munroe shares a story that struck him, which he heard from a Zimbabwean village chief, about a lion among sheep. One day, an old shepherd came across an abandoned lion cub while he was taking his sheep out to pasture. He grew fond of the cub and took him to his farmhouse, treating him like a part

---

11. United Nations Educational, Scientific and Cultural Organization
12. Wikipedia, definition of culture: https://en.wikipedia.org/wiki/Culture

of the herd. After fifteen months, the little cub had become an adolescent lion, but he was behaving just like the sheep, playing and acting like them. He had evolved into one of them. One day, as he was playing by a river with the sheep, a grown lion appeared out of the jungle. The sheep panicked and rushed toward the direction of the farm, afraid to be devoured, and the young lion followed them. One week later, while he had come down to the river with the flock again, once more the beast appeared out of the jungle. Unfortunately, he didn't have enough time to run away at that point. His survival instinct pushed him to try to growl like the beast, but the only noise coming from his gaping jaws was the sound of a sheep. Because of the time spent with his peers, the young lion had lost his true self and had become just like them. He attempted to growl again a second time, but the result was the same. He tried again and after a few attempts, he suddenly heard himself make the same sound as the beast. The old lion headed toward the forest and invited the young lion to follow him, with his eyes. The latter was abruptly faced with a dilemma: to stay in his comfort zone at the safe farm he had known his entire life, or to follow the old lion and become the king of the jungle. After a moment of reflection, he decided to follow his congener, and disappeared with him in the bush.

Take a second and picture the scene. The lion was born to be the king of the jungle: he has the character, power, elegance, and imposing presence. Yet, the time spent at the farm makes him a simple sheep. He's certainly very happy this way, for he has friends, eats as much as he wants, and is protected. However, he's not the one he's meant to be, because living an existence that is not his. The paradox is that he has no clue about this, given none of his peers are by his side to help him realize. His only models of reference are the sheep around him. His life shifts the day his path crosses with one of his congeners, and his eyes open, as if by magic. In contact with the other lion, he sees himself like in a mirror, and becomes aware of who he really is. Two choices then arise: to stay with his friends he grew up with in the surroundings he has always known, or to move on from his past in order to better embrace his new life and take on his true identity.

The main characters of this story are animals, but let's transpose it to our modern world and imagine that the farm symbolizes society, the rules and codes represent culture, and the sheep are the community. If you apply this tale to your life and put yourself in the position of the lion, even just for a few seconds, ask yourself if like him, you are genuinely the person you are supposed to be? Let your imagination flow and allow the burning things or the ones that used to burn deeply in your heart but were extinguished by the hazards, toughness, and constraints of life, to get back to the surface. What comes back to your mind? What are the desires and dreams you gave up on and buried?

You were born at a certain time, you grew up in a country, with its culture, codes, and principles. You were raised either by two or by a single parent, or by a relative, or in a social institution. You grew up in a particular setting and you received a specific education. You had loving, well-intentioned, and attentive parents, who always did their best to make you happy, or, on the contrary, they were indifferent, violent, and dismissive. They were pretty strict, permissive, or flexible, and they had liberal, socialist, far-right, or far-left political views. You attended a public or a private school, or maybe were you home-schooled. The education system gave you knowledge and taught you social values and human rights. You grew up in a big city, a medium-sized town, or a village. You were raised in a detached house or in an apartment, in a quiet or a hectic neighborhood. Your hung out with classmates, or with friends met in your neighborhood or befriended while taking part in sports or cultural activities.

You were a follower, or rather a leader. You learned a trade at a young age, or you undertook graduate studies. You are an entrepreneur, an employee, a jobseeker, a stay-at-home mother or father. You work on your own, or you are surrounded by colleagues all day long. You traveled abroad, or you never left your home country. Your close friends belong to the same socio-professional category as you, or the opposite. You are single, separated, a sole parent, or you are married and you have children.

Each of these elements has participated, to a lesser or greater extent, in making up the person you are today, and is still playing a part. Just like a jigsaw puzzle, every piece is important because they all contribute to composing your profile. They fell into place one by one, year after year, and some have long existed, while others have come into existence more recently. Due to certain life experiences and circumstances, some pieces had to be removed and replaced with others. Still, some turn out to be more important than others because if they were removed and replaced, our life's trajectory would be totally different.

- **Peer pressure**

Writer and motivational speaker Jim Rohn used to say: *"You are the average of the five people you spend the most time with."* He knew how much the ones close to us influence our personality and our mentality. How do your friends, colleagues, and family affect your personality? People do not always realize it immediately, but the social group(s) they belong to influence who they are or become, for social groups bring people together around common characteristics and values. Of course, it all depends on the type of group and the room they make for it in their life. Primary groups are those in which individuals have direct relationships, like families, close friends, and colleagues, among others. Then come the secondary groups that involve more formal and institutional relationships, based on common interests, such as political and labor groups. Each has a distinct identity matching the identity of the whole of its members, so to speak. When someone wants to join a group, they first have to accept its specificities and rules. Some enroll in a selfless way, just because they enjoy interacting with other people, whereas others' motives are driven by the prestige, notoriety, and image of the group in question. In this particular case, the sense of belonging enables them to enjoy a touch of social identity.

- **The influence of trends**

Once ill-considered, tattoos were reserved for certain cultures, circles, or misfits set apart by society. This art started to gain popularity in the mid-90s in France. Originally, tattoos were small Chinese characters, quotes, child's or partner's names, favorite animals, or items and symbols representing a lucky charm. The very first tattoos were reasonably sized and intentionally placed on hidden body spots because they were frowned upon in those days, especially within certain social classes and work environments. Little by little, movie and TV stars also adopted tattoos, as well as music artists, sports personalities, and people working in the fashion industry. The previously discreet tattoos became increasingly visible. Some people started to ink their back, shoulder, upper arm, forearm, or even had the entire body tattooed. The influence of celebrities on their fans, together with the importance of media support, have made it possible to democratize this trend and seduce a large amount of people. All you have to do is stroll down the streets of New York, Paris, and London during the summer, and see how many people are tattooed.

What does this example show? It helps us understand how an epiphenomenon can spread and touch thousands, if not millions of people, from the moment it is disseminated by the media and, above all, conveyed by fairly influential opinion leaders, companies, brands, and entities of all kinds.

4 - The media

Under the Roman Empire, the only communication routes were those of land or water. Delivering information required a certain amount of time. Since then, the technological breakthroughs have tremendously decreased the waiting period, to the point where spreading information is nearly instant. The digital revolution took place in the early 90s and led Man to today's so-called "information age". The quantity of information people are daily exposed to has literally skyrocketed. Every day, we are bombarded by a huge amount of data of all kinds, of all sources, and provided by various mediums. A study conducted by the University of Southern California has estimated that if we compiled the totality of information received daily and put it altogether in a journal, we would receive the equivalent of 174 full newspapers, every day[13]. Of course, the media play a central part on this gigantic chessboard, since not only do they relay information, but they convey social values, customs, and culture. Their reach is such that they don't just influence people in general, but their leaders as well. They can subtly shape one's point of view by presenting the news in one way or another.

---

13. Richard Alleyne, *"Welcome to the information age – 174 newspapers a day"*, published on The telegraph website on February 11, 2011: https://www.telegraph.co.uk/news/science/science-news/8316534/Welcome-to-the-information-age-174-newspapers-a-day.html

Many believe that having power necessarily means to be rich. Undoubtedly, wealth opens up a whole range of possibilities; yet, power doesn't reside that much in having the financial means to purchase whatever we want, but rather in having some influence and control over one or more people. With his or her status and choices, the president of a nation exerts influence over the entire country; still, he or she is far from being the richest person of the nation (except in certain countries). Opinion-makers, organizations, or brands capable of reaching and influencing the masses enjoy much greater power than the ones with money, for they can lead them to behave or think in a particular way.

Summary:

> • **Family:** The family environment plays a huge part in child development, for it is where children build and shape their identity. **There is nothing more powerful on Earth than love, and every human being desperately needs love to feel alive.**
>
> • **Education** focuses on developing social skills and manners by adhering to a given culture, its social codes, rules, and moral values. **Instruction**, on the other hand, consists in passing on knowledge to someone.
>
> • **Society:** UNESCO commonly defines culture as: *"that complex whole which includes knowledge, beliefs, arts, morals, laws, customs, and any other capabilities and habits acquired by a human as a member of society."* **Culture is the people's identity.**
>
> • **The media:** They play a central role in society, for not only do they relay information, but they also convey values, trends, customs, and culture within society. Their scope is such that they don't only influence the public, but the country's leaders as well.

Questions:

- Which important points has this chapter enabled you to understand about your personality?

- What would you like to change about yourself?

- Are you an authentic person, in other words are you the same person inside and out? If not, for what reasons? Is it because you don't like the person you are, or rather for self-protection purposes, like to hide your uneasiness, or to show off a certain appearance and thus be loved by others?

- Do you consider that the family environment you grew up in has enabled you to be a fulfilled person? Otherwise, has it negatively impacted your personality?

- Which particularities inherited from society (values, customs, habits) would you like to ditch today?

- After reading the first part of this book, do you feel you truly are the person you are meant to be at present? If not, why?

This first part has allowed us to measure the role played by our family, education, culture, friends, experiences, era, the media, trends, and society, in our personal development. These actors' field of action is essentially intellectual, and they consequently contribute to shaping the way we think. When we get this, we realize how important choosing the people or the things that directly or indirectly influence us is, because none of them is impartial. They have enough power to influence and change us, whether positively or negatively. Even the book you are holding right now is not neutral. It contains my views and the way I reflect on things. If you agree with its overall content, it means I may somehow exert my influence over you. That's the reason why it is important to know about the author's main motives for writing, as well as the sources he or she learns from. **Every time we accept a new idea, a new trend, a teaching, an opinion, a belief, a theory, or a principle that was not ours originally, we grant their author permission to build, reshape, or change our own point of view, our values, and our ideas.** But I wish to reassure you and make clear that my intentions with you are benevolent. My desire is to share some key advice that has helped me in my own life, and perhaps it will save you time. It is important for me to narrate a portion of my personal story, so that you get a sense of what more or less influenced me at different stages of my life and explains the person I am today. It will therefore be easier for you to comprehend which sources have inspired me to write this book.

In my entire youth, I used to go to church on Sundays. When I was old enough to make my own choices, I preferred to turn my back on God and anything related to Him, assuming my life without Him would be much better. I still believed in God, for I had seen Him intervene several times in my life and that of my entourage in quite tangible ways. However, I found at the time that respecting the biblical precepts of a pious life would be an obstacle to achieving my dreams and to the promising future society was offering me. When I was a teenager, society had taught me that the ingredients of pure happiness were the following: to go to college, live life to the fullest, make some good money, have a nice house and a beautiful car, travel and follow your dreams, and simply be free, living without any constraint. I soon learned that in order to be liked, one had to succeed, show off fancy belongings to be seen, have a decent social status to be respected, money to be happy, and a certain power to dominate. It may not always be expressed in such an explicit way, but overall it is the message disseminated all over the place, like in commercials, movies and TV shows, music videos, magazines, and popular broadcasts. This same message gained momentum the last couple of decades, especially with the advent of the Internet and social networks. For a good fifteen years, I did my best to follow the goals society had presented me as alleged keys to success and happiness. Although I reached some of them, I still didn't feel fully satisfied. I kept living my life without listening to what my heart was attempting to tell me. It was trying to warn me, to help me understand that I was on the wrong path, that like a desert mirage, society had deluded me with fake illusions. A forced sick leave (due to physical exhaustion) led me to put my life on hold and finally take some time to think. You know how human nature works: when everything goes out of control, we bring ourselves to finally look up to the sky. So, this forced break obliged me to lift up my eyes and draw closer to God again. I then realized how mistaken I had been all these years, striving for ephemeral happiness.

While I was convinced to be free, through my way of life, my extensive travels, my knowledge and instruction, I couldn't imagine a single second that by complying with society, I had been molded by it completely. My free will was not as free as I believed, considering most of the ideologies I was relying on to build my personal comprehension and judgments were those instilled by society. The way I was looking at the world was primarily filtered though the lens shaped by society and its various actors, along with my personal history. I needed to take a step back to see things with a different perspective: God's perspective. It became possible when I began to readjust my thoughts to His. This confrontation between my mindset and His thoughts enabled me to shed light on a number of things that did not necessarily seem bad to me before, but which were henceforth appearing as obstacles preventing me from seeing myself the way He was seeing me. These intellectual fortresses were locking my mind into a certain line of thought and keeping me captive with a lifetime misinterpretation of myself. Reading the Bible helped me deconstruct my old thought patterns little by little, by destroying some foundations and rebuilding new ones based on God's thought. This renewal of thought progressively allowed me to be free and discover who I really was. I then understood how erroneous the way I had been picturing life and myself was, but to be able to realize it, I first needed to understand some meaningful things. It is precisely what I wish to share with you in the second part of this book.

SECOND PART

Identity according to God

Chapter 4 – Man according to God

Is Man just a living being made of flesh and blood? The Bible says he is much more than this, for in reality, he's a spiritual being. Both perspectives have to be considered, self-awareness differing from one person to the other, depending on whether they believe in coincidence and theory of evolution, or in God's will instead. In an article published in *Le Monde* newspaper in 2015, France was said to be one of the most atheist countries. It was ranked 4th, after Czech Republic, Japan, and China. Indeed, a survey conducted by the European Commission in 2010 stated that an estimated 40% of the French considered themselves atheists, one third believing in some sort of spirit or superior power1. I personally think God created man and woman and that He's the One assigning them an identity. As a consequence, anyone willing to find their true identity should inevitably draw closer to the Creator, so that He can reveal what He has destined them for. In other words, those who do not know nor believe in Him cannot become the man or the woman created by God by themselves. But let's go back to Genesis, where it all started, in order to understand what God's thought was at Creation.

---

1. Leila Marchand, *"Plus de la moitié des Français ne se réclament d'aucune religion"*, published on Le Monde website on May, 07, 2015: http://www.lemonde.fr/les-decodeurs/article/2015/05/07/une-grande-majorite-de-francais-ne-se-reclament-d-aucune-religion_4629612_4355770.html

- **Origins**

At dusk, King David used to withdraw from the hustle and bustle of the palace and play the harp to compose melodies and psalms, while contemplating the starry sky. He was always captivated by God's greatness and magnificence, when admiring such wonder. In one of his psalms, he wrote: *"I will give thanks to You, for I am fearfully and wonderfully made. Wonderful are Your works, and my soul knows it very well."* (Psalm 139:14). With this simple sentence, he acknowledges that human beings are special creatures with outstanding abilities. In the Book of Genesis, the Bible tells how God created Man. He took the dust of the ground, formed a body, and breathed the breath of life in him. The Bible reads: *"And the Lord God formed man of the dust of the ground, and breathed into his nostrils the breath of life; and man became **a living being**."* (Genesis 2:7). Other translations[2] favor the following wording: *"Man became **a living soul**."* Man is a tripartite being, **he is spirit, he has a soul, and he lives in a body**. The spirit is the vital element of the body, it is the most intimate component of human beings, it is encapsulated in the soul. Well aware of this, the Apostle Paul ended his first letter to the Thessalonians with this greeting: *"Now may the God of peace himself sanctify you completely, **and may your whole spirit and soul and body** be kept blameless at the coming of our Lord Jesus Christ! [3]"*.

---

2. Darby Bible
3. 1 Thessalonians 5:23

The **spirit** consists of conscience, intuition, and communion[4]. It is the part with which one communicates with God. The **soul** comprises intelligence, feelings, and will. It is the seat of personality: man's will, intellect, and emotion all lie in the soul, and it serves as the linking chain between the spirit and the body. It is the entity of the human being[5]. The **body**, for its part, enables man to communicate with the physical world, especially through the five senses. This approach of spirit and soul by no means undermines the function of the brain. Quite the contrary, the brain is considered the control tower of the body, the soul working as a kind of software,

---

4. Watchman Nee, *The Spiritual Man*, 1968, p.20
5. Watchman Nee, *The Spiritual Man*, 1968, p.21 to 23

sending commands to the brain, to which it responds through mental processes. Human beings are no ordinary creatures. The Bible states that they were created in the *image* and *likeness* of God. Originally, God drew inspiration from Himself to create Man. God being Spirit, He made Man spirit by giving him a carnal envelope to interact with the physical world. The book of Genesis tells us how this happened:

> *Let us make man (**'Adam**) in our image (**Tselem**), after our likeness, to rule over the fish of the sea and the birds of the air, over the livestock, and over all the earth itself and every creature that crawls upon it. (Genesis 1:27)*

The Hebrew word used for *"image"* is *"tselem"*, which means image, but also shadow. In my book entitled *"The revelation of God's sons"*, I explain that: "Men must discover their identity in God by getting closer to the source again, in order to fully reflect it, and thus become the shadow of God again. The farther we stand from God, the less we resemble Him, therefore the less we receive God's light and life. The closer we get to God, the more we discover who we are in God[6]". The Hebrew word used for *"Man"* is **Adam**, meaning human, or mankind. The word *human* comes from the Latin word *humanus*, derived from *humus*[7], which means earth. The Earth, where Man is from, translates as **Adamah**. The similarity between *Adam* and *Adamah* establishes a strong connection between Man and the Earth. We find the word *Adamah* when God fashions Man:

---

6. Pascal Malonda, *"The Revelation of God's Sons"*, 2016, p.166
7. Google, Latin & Greek etymology, see: https://sites.google.com/site/etymologielatingrec/home/h/homme

> Then the Lord God formed a man (*'Adam*) from the dust of the ground and breathed into his nostrils the breath of life, and the man became a living being.
> (Genesis 2:7)

In contrast, from the moment God creates woman, the Scriptures draw a distinction between Man referred to as a human being and Man referred to as a male human. The many English translations do not show this subtlety of language, given they use the word "*man*", but the Hebrew text does make the distinction by using the word *Adam* for human being, and the word *Iysh* for man (as a male human). The word used for woman is *Ishshah*[8], coming from *Iysh*, which clearly shows the strong connection between man and woman[9]. This subtlety appears after God creates woman, in the Book of Genesis, chapter 2, verses 21 to 24:

> So the Lord God caused the man (*'Adam*) to fall into a deep sleep; and while he was sleeping, he took one of the man's ribs and then closed up the place with flesh. Then the Lord God made a woman (*'Ishshah*) from the rib he had taken out of the man (*'Adam*), and he brought her to the man (*'Adam*). The man (*'Adam*) said: This is now bone of my bones and flesh of my flesh; she shall be called 'woman' (*'Ishshah*), for

---

8. Marg Mowczko, "*The Human (Ha'adam), Man (Ish) and Woman (Ishshah) in Genesis 2*", see: http://margmowczko.com/human-man-woman-genesis-2
9. http://www.karaitejudaism.org/talks/Ish_and_ishah_relationship.htm

> *she was taken out of man **('Iysh)**.*
> *That is why a man **('Iysh)** leaves his father and mother and is united to his wife **('Ishshah)**, and they become one flesh.*

The Bible defines the first two humans (Adam and Eve) as two beings living in perfect harmony with their Creator. This relationship with God enabled them to know their identity and their role on Earth. Their thoughts were perfectly aligned with those of God, and peace and happiness were prevailing on Earth. Humankind was then living in peace, love, and enjoying immeasurable happiness. There was no violence, no wars, no diseases, no pain, no fear, no famine, no poverty. It was heaven on Earth. Everything changed the day the human will confronted God's will, and a deadly venom infected the human hearts, inducing corrupt thoughts. The intimate bond with God came to an end. Left to their own devices, the thoughts of their hearts have never ceased heading for evil, from that moment on[10]. Society's ills originate from that fateful day when Man's thought was corrupted. Hence, the only way for human beings to understand their role on Earth and reach complete happiness is to recover their initial communion with their Creator.

---

10. "The Lord saw that the wickedness of man was great in the earth, and that every intention of the thoughts of his heart was only evil continually." (Genesis 6:5)

Summary:

- Man is a tripartite being, **he is spirit, he has a soul, and he lives in a body.**

- **The spirit** consists of conscience, intuition, and communion. It is the part with which man communicates with God.

- **The soul** comprises intelligence, feelings, and will. It is the seat of personality: man's will, intellect, and emotion all lie in the soul, and it serves as the linking chain between the spirit and the body. It is the entity of the human being.

- **The body**, for its part, enables man to communicate with the physical world, especially through the five senses.

Chapter 5 – Natural Man and spiritual Man

Several researches on newborns have shown that human beings are born with an innate moral sense. Paul Bloom, a professor of psychology at Yale and author of a book entitled *"Just babies: The origin of the good and evil"*, wrote: *"Babies possess certain moral foundations — the capacity and willingness to judge the actions of others, some sense of justice, gut responses to altruism and nastiness."*[1] In the Bible, we learn that what Paul Bloom refers to as "innate moral sense" was placed by God in every man and woman's conscience so that they could judge what is good or bad by themselves. Everyone is born with this conscience, which makes it possible to instinctively abide by its most elementary principles, as indicated in this verse:

> *For when Gentiles[2] who do not have the law do instinctively the things of the law, these, not having the law, are a law to themselves, in that they show **the work of the law written in their hearts**, their*

---

1. Paul Bloom, *"The Moral Life of Babies"*, see: http://www.nytimes.com/2010/05/09/magazine/09babies-t.html
2. Gentiles usually means a people, nations other than Israel. See: https://www.biblestudytools.com/dictionary/gentiles/

> *conscience bearing witness and their thoughts **alternately accusing or else defending them**, on the day when, according to my gospel, God will judge the secrets of men through Christ Jesus.* (Romans 2:14)[3]

This natural knowledge of what is good or bad gives everyone a chance to respect the framework that is right for them, as well as for others. When we derogate from it, our conscience reprimands and corrects us, to continue benefiting from the protection offered by that framework. Throughout their lives, people develop their own moral values scale (of what is right or wrong). Or course, that scale is based on the education and instruction they receive, along with the rules and principles conveyed by society. When a child grows up and one of society's actors expresses opposing values, an inner fight arises deep inside, for the antagonistic values collide with the ones that already exist in the child's conscience. This fight doesn't cease unless the individual makes up their own choice. If in line with their conscience, a feeling of inner peace settles in, but if not, their conscience's little voice will make itself heard with a warning reminding them what the right way forward is. If despite all this, stubbornness remains, and if the individual repeats the same actions several times, or if they grew up in a place that trivializes certain types of bad behavior, the little voice of conscience will eventually go silent because of the person's deliberate choice of replacing their natural conscience with their own rules and way of looking at things. A mistake widely made by many people is to believe they are free to do whatever they want, without any life consequences

---

3. New American Standard Bible

and repercussions. Author Derek Prince once said: *"People talk about breaking God's laws, that's not true. We don't break God's laws, God's laws break us, if we break them.*[4]*"*

In the same way as there are physical and mathematical laws, there are also spiritual laws. These laws regulate the balance in our world and all of its components. We are not able to fully comprehend how it operates. Proof is that science never stops making new discoveries and breakthroughs. Only the Creator, who is above absolutely everything, knows and understands the instructions and indications He provided Man with. These do not exist in order to imprison him, but rather to protect him, just like a mother and a father stay beside their child when he or she learns to walk, to make sure the child doesn't fall over and doesn't get hurt. The rules and principles intentionally designed by God for human beings may be seen as freedom-killing by some, but in fact they prove to act as protection, for He knows His creation and what is good for it. God is love and His intentions toward humans have always been those of a good Father toward His children. They aim to ensure they enjoy good health, peace, joy, success, well-being and, above all, true freedom. Man's freedom according to God lies in having perfectly aligned thoughts with those of his Creator, for this guarantees him a bright future, and peace.

---

4. Derek Prince, *"Don't give up!"*, YouTube link: https://www.youtube.com/watch?v=liSM3sYRvFQ&t=245s), at min 6:08

1 - Natural Man

Natural man and woman build their comprehension from rational elements, a tiny room being allocated to the spiritual, through their conscience and intuition. Their life is essentially driven by their reasonings, thoughts, emotions, and environment. To describe them, the Apostle Paul uses the word *"fleshy"*, of which the original Greek word is *sarkikos*, which means "governed by mere human nature, not by the Spirit of God"[5]. The human body functions as an intermediary between the inner and the outer world, through the five senses. Sight, sound, touch, smell, and taste receive an impressive amount of information which they transfer to the soul, then in charge of treating and interpreting them. Depending on their usefulness and importance, the soul converts them into intelligible thoughts. Generating a thought can open the door to two possibilities. In the first-case scenario, the thought remains at the information stage, due to its little relevance, and consequently evaporates. In the second case, the thought generated is taken into account, stored in the mind, and results in an action, a word, a reflection, or an emotion. When the same thought occurs several times and is systematically taken into consideration by the individual, it eventually sets in, and becomes a habit. A habit takes place when a thought becomes an integral part of the inner world, because it doesn't need to be treated anymore nor interpreted like the others. Thus, every time it shows up again, it almost automatically triggers the associated action, word, emotion, or behavior. This might justify some of our emotions. Why are some people naturally optimistic while others are paralyzed by fear, or dominated by jealousy or anger?

---

5. Definition of *"Sarkikos"*, see: https://www.biblestudytools.com/lexicons/greek/nas/sarkikos.html

The human body allows passage of everything it hears, sees, and perceives, without ever monitoring it because this responsibility of treating and selecting mainly lies with the soul. Therefore, everything you listen to, look at and touch settles and dwells in you if you give free access to it. The outer world's influence is such that if you don't carefully and thoroughly select the flow of information you receive daily, it eventually ends up governing what you believe, think, and become. Your soul being constantly overwhelmed by all kinds of information, it inevitably needs to analyze what it should keep or not. The sorting process is made according to very personal criteria, such as your values, education, experiences, convictions, culture, successes and failures, desires and fears, dreams and passions. It can also be based on much less personal criteria, but which you have spontaneously assimilated because they are part of society's characteristics. It is your duty to comply with them because they are common to all citizens. This may include the law, customs, values, and codes of conduct shared by the overall community. All the elements you have previously assimilated act as parameters helping you to process and select what you should keep or discard among the countless flow of information, what you can or cannot do, or what you identify as good or bad. Your ultimate discernment therefore builds on your personal criteria, the principles instilled by society, as well as those placed in your conscience.

2 - Spiritual Man

As seen earlier, Man is spirit, he has a soul, and he lives in a body. The Hebrew word for soul is *nephesh*, which means "living being, inner being of man". So, **the soul refers to the personality.** The spirit is the most intimate part of a human being, it is encapsulated in the soul, therefore it cannot communicate with the outer world without passing through the soul first. The soul has a central position in this triunity (spirit-soul-body), in acting as a conductor between the body and the spirit. The soul belongs to both the visible and the invisible world, for it communicates sometimes with the spirit, sometimes with the body. The Creator clothed Man with a carnal envelope, for him to interact with the physical world. Like any physical element, the human body has a beginning, but also an end. It has a limited lifetime, unlike the spirit, which is eternal. The day our body dies, our spirit leaves its earthly shelter in order to head to its final destination. In the same way as someone's identity grants them the right to live and stay in their home country, the same goes in the spiritual world. The identity acquired by the earthly citizen thereby determines the location of their eternal residency. I think you would agree that nobody can invite themselves into a stranger's home and impose their presence on them, without asking for permission first. The same applies to human beings when they die. They can have access to eternity with God, only provided they have known and accepted Him before.

This identity change occurs in the lives of men and women who, at a given time of their existence, have a special encounter with God, and can testify that something tangible just happened. That eye-opening day, they all of a sudden are confident that God is alive. What they had never apprehended before becomes crystal clear, like an evidence. This firm belief leads them to accept Jesus as the Messiah, the Son of God, and admit Him with sincere hearts. THE most extraordinary miracle that could possibly exist in someone's life has just happened. The Bible calls it: **new birth**[6]. It results in **the regeneration of the spirit**. The following Bible passage explains it:

> But when the kindness of God our Savior and His love for mankind appeared, He saved us, not on the basis of deeds which we have done in righteousness, but according to His mercy, **by the washing of regeneration and renewing by the Holy Spirit**, whom He poured out upon us richly through Jesus Christ our Savior, so that being justified by His grace we would be made heirs according to the hope of eternal life. (Titus 3:4-7)

The Greek word for "regeneration" is *paliggenesia*, meaning "new birth, renewal, reproduction, regeneration". The word is often used to denote the restoration of a thing to its pristine state, its renovation[7]. The spirit of man, formerly unfamiliar with God's matters because spiritually dead since the disobedience of Adam and Eve, suddenly revives. This confession invites the Spirit of God to come reside in his spirit, which instantly recreates it. Here is what the Bible says: *"I will give you a new heart and put a new spirit in you; I will*

---

6. New birth is effective to anyone who confesses with their mouth that they accept Jesus Christ as Lord and Savior and give Christ access to their life. The Apostle Paul said: *"If you confess with your mouth the Lord Jesus, and if you believe in your heart that God has risen Him from the dead, you will be saved."* (Romans 10:9)

Source: *The Revelation of God's Sons*, Pascal Malonda
7. Definition of *"paliggenesia"*, see: https://www.biblestudytools.com/lexicons/greek/nas/paliggenesia.html

remove from you your heart of stone and give you a heart of flesh." (Ezekiel 36:26). The new birth thus restores man and woman to their initial position, as son and daughter of God, as they were at Creation. In the beginning, they used to think, speak, and behave as wished by the Creator, for their hearts were in perfect harmony with His thought.

- **The sons and daughters of God**

It is important to make a distinction between a believer and a child of God. The Bible calls "children of God" those whose spirit has been renewed by the power of the Holy Spirit. The Holy Spirit henceforth resides in their spirit, which allows Him to communicate with God. The life of the child of God is no longer led by their five senses, emotions, environment, or human reasonings, as the natural man and woman can be (that is, the ones who haven't met God personally), but by God's voice, too. This privilege is reserved for the children of God, as written by the Apostle Paul in his letter to the Romans: *"For all those who are led by the Spirit of God are the children of God"* (Romans 8:14).

To understand the difference between a person who was born again and one who was not, let's look at the following diagrams:

Figure 1. Person who was not born again

Personality (soul) **+** Conscience (spirit) **=** Personal identity

The first diagram shows a person who doesn't know God. The image they have about themselves is mainly based on what society and its various actors have conveyed, and on their encounters and personal experiences. God can talk to them through their spirit with some intuitions and dreams, however this doesn't allow them to know God nor who they really are.

Figure 2. Person who was born again

The second diagram shows a person who was born again. The way they see God and themselves is different because it is influenced by the Holy Spirit, who resides in them and conveys God's thought. Here is what the Scriptures say about it:

> *For what man knows the things of a man except the spirit of the man which is in him?* ***Even so no one knows the things of God except the Spirit of God.*** *Now we have received, not the spirit of the world, but the Spirit who is from God, that we might know the things that have been freely given to us by God.* (1 Corinthians 2:11-12)

However, the first years spent walking with God are not that easy, for a sort of inner fight occurs between the spirit, which is renewed, and the soul, which is not. While the renewed spirit is naturally attracted to the things of God, the soul, for its part, still has the memories of the past emotions, experiences, habits, and reasonings. If the Bible states that: *"Therefore if anyone is in Christ, he is a new creature; the old things passed away; behold, new things have come."* (2 Corinthians 5:17), it is still necessary to destroy some fortresses, as we will see in the next chapter.

In creating Man, God established a hierarchy between the spirit, the soul, and the body, so that the spirit is superior to the soul, and the soul is superior to the body. **As long as the spirit of Man was perfectly aligned with God's thought, God's principles could be followed on Earth, as if God was ruling through His creation**. The day Adam and Eve disobeyed and were separated from God, this order reversed. Far from His thought, the body surpassed the soul, and the soul surpassed the spirit, which caused the overthrow and domination of the outer world over the inner world. Ever since that day, humankind has been dominated by the sinful nature that resides in the human body, and instrumentalizes it every time the flesh overpowers the soul. Sin lives in the flesh and exerts a force on the body, which in turn exerts it on the soul, pushing it to accomplish things that are *contrary to God's will*. For many people, it is difficult to realize that the way they think, behave, or live is contrary to God's will, either because they do not believe in Him or because they don't know what His will is. As a matter of fact, they don't even feel they are doing anything wrong, given they comply with the social rules, and behave like the majority of people. Yet, as long as humans are on Earth, their carnal nature pushes them to seek their own interests and focus on themselves. This triggers envy, selfishness, avarice, pride, jealousy, wrath, debauchery, and much more. Fortunately, the Spirit of God enables the sons and daughters of God to control their flesh, by re-establishing the hierarchy between their spirit, their soul, and their body, and by making the thought of God available to them.

3 - Has society taken God's place?

Jesus said: *"You shall love the Lord your God with all your **heart**, and with all your **soul**, and with all your **strength**, and with all your **mind**; and your neighbor as yourself"* (Luke 10:27). Every word used is fundamental, for the **heart** is the vital center of Man, being the seat of the physical and spiritual life. The **soul** refers to emotions, feelings, and intellect. The **mind**, for its part, refers to the internal dialogue that takes place inside every person. **Strength** symbolizes the person's mental and physical energy. Since Man moved away from God, he has replaced Him with his mind, wisdom, values, principles, knowledge, and intelligence. **When God is not in the center, there has to be something or someone holding His position, for it is how Man was conceived.**

Food can meet the body's needs, relationships and family delight the soul, but only God can bring the light and the life people need with their whole being. Try to fill a petrol car with diesel fuel and it won't be long before it breaks down. The same goes for humans. The ills faced by society are mainly due to the fact that people, for the most part, are self-centered and tend to strive for their own wellbeing, thus forgetting their spiritual self. They are unware of this because they simply apply what they have been taught. Jesus once said: *"Man shall not live by bread alone, but by every word that comes from the mouth of God."* (Matthew 4:4) Through these simple words, He revealed that the secret of man and woman doesn't lie in earthly foods but in spiritual food, that is to say the Word of God communicating life to their whole being.

Society is an entity that has a mind, a voice, and a power. It has recreated the framework designed by God originally, by redefining itself the rules and values of its members, by ruling on Man's origins, by determining the meaning of life and the reasons why Man is on Earth. The overall functioning of society is henceforth articulated around the enforcement of the rules, laws, principles, values, and answers it has itself established. It somehow took God's place in replacing His instructions with some of its own. It influences the general population via leading actors such as the State, big institutions, the media, large companies, industries, banks, influential spheres, political parties, research and science, not to mention the opinion-makers.

Does it mean that what society has to offer is bad?

Not at all, but each of these fields being governed by men and women who, like you and me, also have their own way of thinking, interests, rules and values… you will probably agree that what they propose is everything but neutral, considering it is inevitably swayed by their personality. Questioning all you have learned so far or who you are is out of the question, but realizing some inconvenient hidden truths is important. In the Information Age, influencing others is an art and one of the most powerful skills. When a major actor finds or initializes a new idea or trend, he or she endeavors to share it with the population, through the media and multiple communication channels. After a while, the novelty ends up under the spotlight, being seen, heard, and read by a large audience. Some will accept and incorporate it, while others choose to ignore it when it seems useless to them, or simply don't buy it. The effects on the public can vary a lot. Some trends are just a passing fad and disappear shortly after being launched. Other tendencies, although incorporated by multitudes, do not cause deep structural shifts among the population. In contrast, there are also much more impactful trends, influential enough to modify certain values, customs, and even lifestyles. This phenomenon made the modern world we know and live in now. It applies to the *"good"* and the *"bad"* things at the same time. I'm intentionally using quotation marks because as discussed while studying the thought process, the way we estimate a good or a bad thing clearly depends on one another's opinion. Over the centuries, some rules and values have disappeared in favor of new ones. Some points of view and behaviors formerly considered on the fringes of society are now accepted, if not encouraged. Others, initially regarded as honorable, are now seen as old-fashioned.

Still, history has repeatedly taught us that because a country, a political party, an organization, a community, or a society proposes some rules, laws, and principles, or defends some values and encourages some behaviors, it doesn't automatically guarantee that it is beneficial for the population. Anatole France once said: *"If fifty million people say a foolish thing, it is still a foolish thing."* Several citizens associations, consumer organizations, or NGOs such as Wikileaks have indeed revealed that some laws, decisions, and regulations which prima facie were beneficial for citizens were in fact hiding other motives of rather financial or ideological nature.

- **Social phenomena**

There was an age when tobacco was viewed positively in society. At that time, smoking in public places was permitted, if not promoted. Then the first studies on the harmful effects of active smoking were released, followed by those on passive smoking. In response to that issue, governments timidly added the topic to the many public health discussions. Despite all this, tobacco still kills more than 7 million people each year[8]. This example perfectly illustrates how something seen as "good" by society at a certain point can become the exact opposite over time. It also highlights that when a certain

---

8. World Health Organization (WHO), *"Tobacco"*, published in March 2018: http://www.who.int/news-room/fact-sheets/detail/tobacco

conduct is adopted by the masses, it doesn't necessarily mean it is reliably "good" for people, since it can prove to be extremely damaging, years later.

Summary:

- Having a natural knowledge of right and wrong allows people to respect the framework that works best for them, but also for others.

- The life of natural man and woman is mainly driven by their reasonings, thoughts, emotions, and environment.

- Born again spiritual man and woman are guided by the Spirit of God. The Bible calls children of God those whose spirit has been renewed by the power of the Holy Spirit.

- The overall functioning of society is henceforth articulated around the enforcement of the rules, laws, principles, values, and answers it has itself established. It somehow took God's place in replacing His instructions with some of its own.

Questions:

- Do you consider yourself a natural or a spiritual man or woman? Which elements make you believe so?

- Who runs your life? Yourself, society, or the Spirit of God?

- Do you tend to spontaneously follow new trends? If so, would you say that you are easily influenced?

Chapter 6 – Freedom

Proudly standing at the entrance to the New York Harbor, the Statue of Liberty symbolizes freedom for the United States, but also for the rest of the world. In France, the motto of the Republic — *"Liberty, Equality, Fraternity"* — is engraved on the pediments of the city halls and public buildings. The countries which have faced war tend to fondly recall how important freedom is, because they are aware of its cost, and because they have acquired it at the sacrifice of human lives. What does liberty represent in today's society? For many, it means being able to move and act as they wish, as long as it doesn't encroach on the freedom of others. As the adage goes, *"Your liberty ends just where my nose begins"*. In some countries, citizen control is exerted with threat and fear, whereas in other places it is way subtler, with leaders aware that having the masses accept and assimilate the norms and values which condition who they are, how they think, and how they act, works effectively enough. How many people are convinced they are free, just because they can move around, consume, and act as they wish, without imagining a second that their education, instruction, and convictions actually lock themselves into thinking and behaving in a certain way?

There are also the ones who, in spite of being physically free, are trapped in a sort of emotional prison. The subtlety of mental and spiritual captivity resides in the fact that it cannot be detected at first glance. Whether an addiction, a depression, or any negative feeling, it silently lurks out of sight until brought to light. A person trapped in their own mind always tends to act and make decisions at odds with their true nature. Every time, making these choices leads them to the same complicated situations that overtake them, due to their complete helplessness. One of the very first steps to freedom involves identifying the principles, rules, and values which you have assimilated, and seeing them as a whole in order to make them fit with your personality. This will make you able to measure to what extent they impact your life and evaluate whether they suit you, or if you feel they hinder you deep inside. On this basis, you might feel the need or the urge to change some of them, or instead you will remain the same.

Real freedom is not so much about what we can do, but rather what we are. It is only accessible to those who discover who they really are deep inside, before the social and societal factors began to mold their identity and, above all, those who strive to become so. If that is your case, making this decision will require courage. You may need a certain time before you feel ready to question and reconsider the things you always thought right about yourself, which in fact are presently keeping you from understanding who you really are. Typically, this process is much more time-consuming and painful for the ones with low self-esteem, because they forcibly need to deconstruct the lies about them in order to rebuild themselves by resting on the truth. Without this period of self-reflection, their mindset can mislead them by making them believe they are incapable or totally fine the way they are, or that the problem doesn't really come from themselves, but from others. At some point of their life, many men and women have to take the necessary time to reconsider their existence, otherwise they risk missing out on it completely.

I once attended a conference in the US, during which Jon Ponder, an ex-offender, was recounting how he founded the non-profit organization *Hope for Prisoners*[1], because he was committed to helping former prisoners reenter and effectively function in mainstream society, once released from jail. With his partners, he developed a program that aims at helping those willing to change their lifestyle and behavioral patterns, regain self-confidence, build the necessary skills for job placement, and learn to take care of their family. This project was warmly welcomed by the prison community, for many studies have shown that a lot of detainees go back to jail very shortly after being released, quite often for the same offence. Indeed, despite being physically free, they remain imprisoned in their own mind because they still have the same mentality, habits, pitfalls, acquaintances, that is to say, the same mindset. *Hope for Prisoners'* programs prove to be very successful: actually, the vast majority of participants do not go back to prison, since their vision of life has changed. Those programs enable them to understand that whatever they did in the past, they deserve a second chance and they are valuable, only their bad choices formerly led them to a dead end. It is therefore their entire responsibility to decide to get rid of the bad habits holding them captive. To this end, they are offered vocational trainings, *leadership* courses with mentoring programs, and it also involves reuniting and restoring relationships with their loved ones. Thus, they become fully aware of the importance of thinking and acting differently to have a better life, and that true liberty primarily begins in the head and in the heart.

---

1. See website of the Hope for Prisoners organization: https://hopeforprisoners.org

The Bible tells the story of Moses the patriarch, who also happened to confront his own self-image. While he was picturing himself in a certain way due to his personal story, God was in fact seeing him very differently. Let's look at his story, so we understand why it is sometimes necessary to destroy our misperceptions about ourselves.

1 - Moses: "Who am I?"

Who am I? That is the question Moses asks God in the book of Exodus, chapter 3, when God requests him to go liberate the children of Israel from Egypt, where they have been enslaved for 430 years. Moses vehemently refuses because he thinks he is not good enough. At the time, he's just a shepherd, and he believes he lacks legitimacy to go unto Pharaoh and ask him to set the Israelites free. God insists and tries to reassure him, explaining that He will stay by his side, but Moses persists. Then follows an anthological conversation between God and Moses, during which God tells Moses how He sees him. Moses's position remains firm, which causes God's anger. At His insistence, Moses eventually gives in and accepts to go to Egypt. The rest of the narrative evidences that not only did a totally unconfident Moses successfully accomplish the mission entrusted by God, but he is now considered one of the greatest leaders in Biblical history. How could this shepherd lead more than two million people? Let's have a closer and more detailed look at his story in order to understand the change that took place in him, and the way he was predestined to become such a leader.

- **Moses's early days**

Immediately after birth, God saves Moses from death. While his mother is constrained to leave him in a basket placed by the river to save his life, God touches the heart of Pharaoh's daughter, who adopts Moses and treats him like her own son. He should have died, he could have lived as a slave with his people, but instead he finds himself growing up in Pharaoh's palace, receiving princely education. As he gets older, he becomes aware of his real people's living conditions, and seeing them abused and enslaved saddens him because he knows what freedom is, thanks to his status. Little by little, anger and outrage settle in him and push him to commit murder when one day, he comes across an Egyptian beating up a Hebrew, and irrevocably kills the former. It surely isn't the first time he sees such violence, but at that moment he just cannot hold back his anger. The next day, he witnesses another fight, between two Hebrews that time, and while he tries to talk some sense into them, one of the two says: *"Who made you ruler and judge over us? Are you thinking of killing me as you killed the Egyptian?"* (Exodus 2:14). On hearing these words, Moses realizes that the news about the incident has seemingly been disclosed. Panic-stricken and fearing for his life, he flees Egypt and takes refuge in the land of Midian. There, he sits down beside a well and sees shepherds chasing women who came to draw water for their flock. The women are the seven daughters of Jethro, namely the priest of Midian. Moses comes to their rescue and waters their flock. When they return to their father, they tell him what just happened: *"An Egyptian rescued us from the shepherds, he even drew water for us and watered the flock."* (Exodus 2:19). To express his gratitude, the priest asks his daughters to find and invite Moses to have something to eat. Moses accepts and stays with them. Jethro gives his daughter Zipporah to Moses in marriage. Moses becomes a shepherd and spends his time looking after his father-in-law's animals. He is then forty years old. Forty years later, seeing His people's sufferings and tears, and upon hearing the cries of despair that reached Him, God decides to send Moses to Egypt to liberate them. This is what He said to Moses:

> *"And now the cry of the Israelites has reached me, and I have seen the way the Egyptians are oppressing them. So now, go. I am sending you to Pharaoh to bring my people the Israelites out of Egypt."* But Moses said to God, **"Who am I that I should go to Pharaoh and bring the Israelites out of Egypt?"** *And God said, "I will be with you. And this will be the sign to you that it is I who have sent you: when you have brought the people out of Egypt, you will worship God on this mountain."*
> (Exodus 3:9-12)

Moses's answer to God is surprising: *"**Who am I that I should go to Pharaoh and bring the Israelites out of Egypt?**"*. Paradoxically, the same Moses, who earlier was ready to rebel alone against the Egyptian empire, and who had managed to scare away several shepherds, had lost the confidence and intrepidness of his. Yet, upon arriving in the Midian, Jethro's daughters had mistaken him with an Egyptian, certainly because of his attire, but not solely. Moses had the bearing, the imposing presence, and the aura of a prince. However, the time spent in the desert with the flock had overshadowed his predisposition for leadership. The question he then asked

God is of primary importance because it proves Moses didn't know who he was anymore and why God would choose him over someone else.

The story of Moses is full of life lessons because once again, it evidences how influential the environment is on someone's identity. In the Acts of the Apostles, Stephen says about Moses: *"Moses was educated in all the wisdom of the Egyptians and was powerful in speech and action."* (Acts 7:22) Moses was an influential and bold man who didn't scare easily, the proof is that he murdered the Egyptian without batting an eye. When he killed him, Moses thought his peers would side with him and revolt, but instead of seizing the opportunity, they did not react because they didn't understand Moses's move. This misunderstanding is due to the fact that they did not interpret his act the way he would have liked, because their state of mind was different. On the one hand stands a man convinced he can beat the Egyptians because he knows what he's capable of, and on the other hand there is a people that, although much stronger and outnumbering the Egyptian people, dare not revolt because of their slave mentality which forces them into fear and submissiveness. There are obviously two dissimilar states of mind here, two opposing systems of thought.

- **Deconstruction**

God shows Moses the wonders he will have to perform before Pharaoh to convince him he well and truly comes on His behalf, and thus persuade him to liberate the people. God provides responses to each of his arguments, in order to debunk the misconceptions and false beliefs that were assimilated by his system of thought after all his time spent in the desert, which undoubtedly prevent him from seeing himself the way he really is, henceforward. God endeavors to deconstruct the reasonings that block and paralyze Moses, one by one, so that he remolds his self-image by restoring his lost self-confidence. Moses needs to ditch his shepherd mentality, even though he will need it again later when it comes to taking care of his people; but for the time, he has to regain the charisma and leadership which are his trademarks, not only because he's the future leader of the people, but also because he's meant to represent God before Pharaoh. Despite all this, Moses has so completely lost confidence that he refuses to journey there, invoking his stuttering disorder. Exasperated, God says to him: *"Who has made man's mouth? Who makes him mute, or deaf, or seeing, or blind? Is it not I, the Lord? Now therefore go, and I will be with your mouth and teach you what you shall speak."* (Exodus 4:11-12) Moses eventually surrenders and goes to Egypt.

With God's help, he manages to free his Hebrew brothers. When they arrived in Egypt, they were only seventy, and four hundred and thirty years later, they are over two million people. As they just arrive in the desert, Moses temporarily goes his own way to the top of a mountain to receive God's instructions, where he will then spend forty days. Simultaneously, the Israelites, impatient to see Moses again, decide to make a golden calf to worship it. After witnessing extraordinary miracles in Egypt, including the Red Sea's splitting in two, they forget the living God who delivered them out of Pharaoh's hand, and make a golden calf for themselves. With this act, they replicate an Egyptian custom that consists in adoring handmade items by attributing certain powers and properties to them. When Moses comes down from the mountain, he is so highly exasperated that he breaks the Tables of the Law. Because of all the years living under slavery, the people needs to change the way they think, otherwise they are likely to reproduce the rules, traditions, and customs learned from the Egyptians, once settled in the Promised Land. For this purpose, God gives the Israelites some laws that will allow them to deconstruct the intellectual, traditional, and customary walls that were erected during all those years, so they can build new ones according to His thought. It is interesting to point out that leaving Egypt took them one day, but freeing themselves from the grip of Egypt took forty years.

2 - The renewal in humans

- **Intellectual and emotional renewal**

It is sometimes necessary to unwind and listen to your heartbeat to make sure you are on the right path or, on the contrary, to identify whether you are missing the whole point of your existence. Every individual willing to ascertain they are on the right track, or looking to readjust their motion, will have to slow down the pace sooner or later, and proceed to self-reflection and introspection. For many, it is necessary, if not essential, especially those harmed by life's hardships, who need to gather strength to get back on their feet and jump back into the race. This much-needed break enables you to audit your life, for like the current of the ocean pushes the boats far away when they are not strongly docked, the rhythm of life often pushes us far from what's deeply enshrined in our heart. Some people achieve this pretty easily, however it can be an extremely demanding exercise for others, because some suppressed memories they wish were completely erased tend to resurface. Although many years have passed, time is like static within themselves. Even so, they did their best to meet society's expected requirements by studying, working, being in a relationship or getting married, buying a house, making friends, and having a social life. Other people regularly set themselves new goals, they strive to fulfill their dreams and to build a successful career, which ignites passion and happiness in them, simply because it matches the genuine fondnesses of their heart. However, despite their best efforts, these activities do not favorably answer the existential questions of their soul. Some give up living like this, finding meaning in their life through the various actions they happen to pursue, while others don't have the strength to keep deluding themselves, and in time, too exhausted to carry on like this, they eventually get down on one knee.

Many see depression as the illness of the soul. Globally, more than three hundred million people of all ages suffer from depression, including three million in France. Every year, numerous people seek medical treatment with a view to feeling better about themselves. Some choose to go to therapy, not only to "put the pain on pause", but also and especially to identify the causes, to carry out some sort of restoration work with the patient, and help them say goodbye to their constant malaise.

The disciplines of psychology and psychiatry as well as neuroscience have for years been concentrating their studies on understanding how the mind works, having well discerned that it plays a major role in the functioning of humans. Sigmund Freud, considered the father of modern psychology, also understood the importance of researching the mental processes behind a thought or a behavior. Psychoanalysis focuses on studying how the soul works, although not directly referred to with this word, due to its overly religious connotation. The terms *psyche* and *psychic* are more commonly used, and they come from the Greek word *psukhé*, which means soul. During his dedicated research time, Sigmund Freud found out three levels of consciousness: the conscious, preconscious, and unconscious. He developed several theories around those three levels, some being disputed later, if not denied by some of his successors who expressed reservations on his studies, especially regarding the role of the unconscious mind, as well as repression. The comprehension of these three levels has subsequently progressed over time, particularly with additional disciplines such as philosophy, psychology, or psychiatry, which shed significant light on how the soul works. These three levels of consciousness are typically presented through the metaphor of an iceberg, as shown in the diagram below. The term "subconscious", meaning "below the level of consciousness", is widely preferred in psychology, whereas the term "preconscious" is rather used in psychiatry.

The three levels of consciousness:

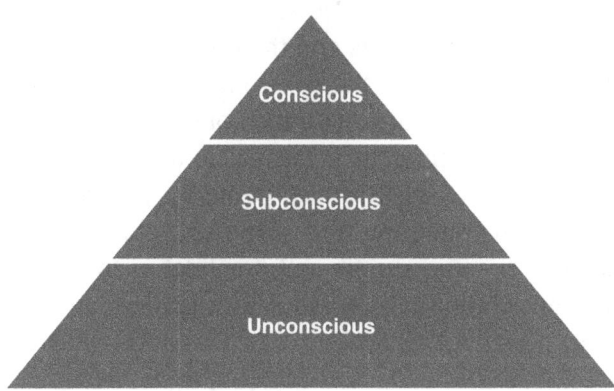

- **The conscious mind** contains all that we see, hear, feel, perceive, know, and understand, and as the name suggests, all that we are aware of. The conscious mind communicates with both the inner world (thoughts) and the outer world (words, gestures).

- **The subconscious mind** contains the information we have memorized, which is easily retrievable when we think or concentrate. Some people like to describe its role by comparing it to that of a computer RAM (random access memory).

- **The unconscious mind** is a reservoir of accumulated memories stored since childhood, which are outside of our conscious awareness. It includes knowledge, experiences, life events, but also unacceptable or unpleasant wounds and trauma. The unconscious mind plays a key role in our life because the pieces of information it contains contribute to making who we are, to the extent that they greatly influence our thoughts, attitude, and behavior.

The three minds — conscious, subconscious, and unconscious — work together. The subconscious plays a pivotal role between the conscious and the unconscious, similarly to that of the soul between the spirit and the body. Indeed, the subconscious collaborates with the conscious and the unconscious at the same time, as if they were arranged in a sort of triunity. Doctor Joseph Murphy wrote several books on the subject and illustrated the role of the conscious and the subconscious with some simple and practical examples. Here is one of them, comparing our soul to a garden, and us to the gardener:

> *An excellent way to get acquainted with the two functions of your mind is to look upon your own mind as a garden. You are a gardener, and you are planting seeds (thoughts) in your subconscious mind all day long, based on your habitual thinking.*[2]

---

2. Joseph Murphy, *"The power of your subconscious mind, Law of attraction Haven"*

This example clearly shows the close collaboration between the conscious and the subconscious. On a daily basis, the conscious receives all sorts of information, intellectualized in the form of thoughts, and the pieces of information that feed the conscious the most end up memorized in the subconscious, as an integral part of it. Every time we learn something new, the information is stored in our subconscious mind. This occurs for example when a child learns to ride a bicycle, or when an adult learns to drive a car. During the learning phase, the moves and reflexes are hesitant, but after a lot of practice, they become automatic, and neither the child nor the adult necessarily needs to stay focused while riding the bike or driving the car.

The subconscious mind cannot judge what is good or bad, right or wrong, or even choose what to keep or not. It simply receives what the conscious mind transfers to it, without having a say. This is how attitudes, mental patterns, automatisms, good and bad habits are formed.

A couple I'm friends with left France in 2016 to achieve their dream of opening an orphanage, in order to house the disadvantaged children of Kinshasa's streets. After a year, they welcomed four boys aged ten to fifteen. The early days were a bit hectic because the young teenagers were feeling deprived of the freedom they always knew on the streets. From then on, they had to comply with the house rules by participating in the household chords, making their bed, tidying up their bedroom, listening to and respecting the educators, avoiding fights, talking without swearing, and working in school. The first months were quite chaotic because the boys were continually challenging the rules, causing tensions and conflicts. One of them even decided to go back and live on the streets. Despite their sadness, the couple remained firm with the rules they had defined, and little by little their efforts started to pay off. They progressively noticed a positive change in the children's conduct, marked by their spontaneous contribution around the house and their respecting the household instructions. Admittedly, it took a while because it was necessary to first destroy the former mentality they had acquired on the streets, which was making them prisoners of a bad attitude and a negative behavior. For this transformation to be effective and lasting, the changes had to be made at two levels: intellectually and emotionally. They needed to let go of all the emotional wounds they had accumulated and inherited from the past, which they were carrying in the present like burdensome luggage. Abandon, violence, poverty, lack of love, were all internal wounds strongly rooted in their subconscious and unconscious minds. Getting rid of them was mandatory, for they were impacting their demeanor negatively. The couple and educators' role consisted in helping the teenagers discover who they really were, beyond their past experiences actually distorting the image they had about themselves. The outcome of being in a healthy and quiet environment, surrounded by caring and considerate people loving them as they were, helped them open up and build trust. This goodwill was one of the first steps toward transformation. They emerged as new individuals the day they became convinced that they were valuable, and most importantly, that they were loved.

- **Spiritual renewal**

When we take the discoveries made in psychology and cognitive science to a biblical level, we see some passages of the Holy Scriptures from a very different angle. Thus, when the Apostle Paul asks the believers to be "transformed by the renewal of their mind", he invites them to change their perspectives by acquiring some new knowledge, and by reconsidering some of their actual beliefs. On a neurological level, these actions result in creating or modifying the pre-existing mental patterns by changing the neural connections. Here is Paul's advice:

> *Do not be conformed to this world, but **be transformed by the renewal of your mind**, that by testing you may discern what is the will of God, what is good and acceptable and perfect.* (Romans 12:2)

We have long thought that since the mind and intelligence are intangible, the renewal mentioned by the Apostle Paul was only taking place intellectually. **Thanks to neuroscience, we now know that when we transform the way we think, the change that occurs is not just mental, but also cerebral.** Paul urged the Roman believers to seek to renew their minds, being aware that what they had learned from the Roman culture was preventing them from discerning God's will. In other words, the customs, rites, habits, and traditions of the Roman Empire were keeping them in a system of thought, blocking their metamorphosis. It is no coincidence that the Apostle Paul later used the word *fortress*, namely a physical term, to describe an intangible thought. In his Second Letter to the Corinthians, Paul intentionally used that word to depict the false beliefs and misconceptions people were subject to, at the time. He purposely chose that powerful symbol, for since there was a fortress in Corinth then, he knew it would be easier for contemporary men and women to understand his thought. The passage goes as follows:

> *For the weapons of our warfare are not of the flesh, but divinely powerful for the **destruction of***

fortresses. We are destroying *speculations and every lofty thing* raised up against the knowledge of God, and we are taking *every thought* captive to the obedience of Christ, and we are ready to punish all disobedience, whenever your obedience is complete. (2 Corinthians 10:4)

The Greek word used for "destroy" is *kathaireo,* which literally means "to pull down, to demolish the subtle reasonings of opponents likened to a fortress[3]". Paul opts for some usually relating to buildings terminology to express how the culture of the time, the worship of false gods, as well as traditions had erected some impregnable fortresses around the believers' souls, making it difficult to understand the gospel he was preaching. In Paul's mind, the word fortress refers to the spiritual strongholds that settle in some doctrines, ideologies, and beliefs. Hence, they enable Satan and his demons to operate and to have dominion over people and organizations, by exerting control through their thoughts and opinions. The solution Paul puts forward consists in wiping out their reasonings and false beliefs, as we would demolish a fortress, but using the suitable weapons accordingly. Indeed, he automatically puts the fleshy (human) weapons aside, otherwise it would result in a word battle like: wisdom against wisdom, philosophy against philosophy, arguments against arguments. But, Man being spirit, all he needs is a **revelation**. This occurs when the spiritual weapons, namely the Word of God in addition to prayers, successfully remove the veil covering his mind, and thus allow the light of revelation to penetrate and convince him. That is why the Bible says: *"Then you will*

---

3. Definition of *"kathaireo",* see: https://www.biblestudytools.com/lexicons/greek/nas/kathaireo.html

know the truth, and the truth will set you free." (John 8:32). Because when the spirit is enlightened, so are the entire body and the soul.

One of my friends was an atheist. Having studied various theological ideas, his research had confirmed his views: according to him, God did not exist, and the current state of society was only convincing him all the more. He liked to debate with believers to prove them wrong regarding their beliefs, intending to persuade them those were completely abstract, and based on nothing serious. He took it to heart so much that at some point, he started to read the Bible in order to counteract the Christians on their own turf. One day, without being really able to explain it, he felt the need to go to church, out of curiosity. He didn't want to go to just any church since he had mocked some of his believer colleagues: he simply didn't want to bump into them. One of his friends advised him to join a group of Christians that used to get together on Sunday mornings in a hotel. He went there, and the message of the day was about love. He found the way everything was addressed pretty interesting, so he decided to give it another go. Every time he attended the mass again, he was nicely surprised with the announced message, but also with the interactions he could have with the people there, at the end of the service. A Sunday morning, during the praise, some tears started running down his cheeks for no particular reason. Quite puzzled, he hid his face, so nobody would see him, and he tried to stop crying, but without success. When he left, he looked up to the sky, and tears started flowing again. When observing trees, birds, and nature in general, he would cry again. He had the impression to have wide-open eyes, as if the way he was looking at the things he'd always known was suddenly different. This strange experience lasted a week.

The revelation had come to overthrow his amassed knowledge and pierce his spirit. From then on, he was convinced of God's existence.

- **Your fortresses**

Some of your fortresses have surreptitiously erected in you, year after year, brick after brick. You're not always aware of them because they are a part of your personality, and they have become natural with time. They are strongly anchored in your subconscious and unconscious mind, and they drive your thoughts and actions. Some are necessary, for they protect you against the external enemies that may want to harm you by bombarding you with ideologies, doctrines, principles, and values that contradict yours. Somehow, they keep you safe from what's likely to hurt and change you without your consent. While some fortresses are directly tied to your life experiences, others were raised following some painful events, and now act as a bulwark that preserves you so that you don't get affected by these things anymore. To this end, they protect your integrity by barricading your "SELF", allowing only the useful and necessary elements to be filtered. Thus, they block what your brain identifies as futile or dangerous for you. Just like the body, your fortresses are there to guard your soul. However, some fortresses can also mislead you, and keep you from comprehending what is good for your life, by negatively influencing your discernment and understanding abilities. For example, you may see some points of view or actions as absurd, just because you are unable to apprehend them with your intelligence and reasoning, and you might perceive some behaviors and opinions as good when they are not, because you have accepted them as such. It is really difficult and even nearly impossible to be fully objective, for our vision of things is inextricably linked to our personality and personal experiences.

Your spiritual fortresses are sometimes so deeply rooted that they block your inner renewal. Spiritual transformation still occurred during the new birth (for those who were born again), but then it is time for the soul (thoughts, emotions, and mind) to be transformed in turn by the power of the Holy Spirit, who works through our spirit. Reading the Bible, praying, praising, fasting, remaining in the presence of God, all bring the necessary elements to help the spirit strengthen up and gradually overpower the soul.

Since your thoughts and actions are influenced by your subjectivity, your may wonder how to be sure that the way you look at your life is completely accurate and objective. Every individual has their own life story, experiences, and knowledge, and what makes a people's richness is the diversity of personalities, characters, and opinions. Your subjectivity certainly built up over your personal history, but not only. As discussed earlier, it was also influenced by what society (through different bodies of power and influence) has instilled in you.

In the end, the outer world is just the reflection of the inner universe of humankind, and the state of our modern societies is in fact the shadow of what's secretly happening in Man's heart.

The only way to fairly comprehend the world, other people, and ourselves, is by looking through the Bible, for although it was written by Man's hand, his source of inspiration is none other than God Himself[4]. The wisdom, advice, values, and principles administered in the Bible are not for the benefit of someone in particular or of a corporation or any pressure group, but in both your and my own interests. Those who understand and apply this principle in their daily life have a truthful way to see the world and themselves, because they then see and grasp things with another perspective: God's perspective. Consequently, they can successfully discern what is good or bad, true or false, useful or useless. This ability enables them to be stable, therefore they don't end up being bounced around, manipulated by the fashions and the few influencers who make the latest trends.

3 - The various sources that feed the thoughts

Diverse sources feed our thoughts. When you discover them, you will better understand where the ideas crossing your mind all day actually come from. Some are brilliant and full of joy, love, wisdom, and humor, they make you feel in a good mood and brighten up your day. Others, on the other hand, are weird, dull, and dark, they overwhelm you like a lead blanket. Rest assured that they don't come up out of nowhere: they all have a point of origin, and it is the emitter behind them that decides on their content. Like a sender mails a letter with a message to an addressee, the source behind your thoughts also conveys an intelligible message to you. Let's have a look at the various sources responsible for your thoughts.

---

[4]. "All Scripture is inspired by God and profitable for teaching, for reproof, for correction, for training in righteousness (…)." (2 Timothy 3:16)

- **Oneself**

    A portion of our thoughts comes from our reflection, imagination, ideas, and emotions of the day. They are a part of the inner world we have built over the years, from our birth to today. They shape up from our personality traits, education and instruction, knowledge, experiences, culture, and from our genuine temper (cheerful, introverted, passionate, calm, etc.).

- **The environnent**

    Some of our thoughts originate from the information our environment delivers to us, and they are detected by our senses. The setting we evolve in, whether professional, friends, family, or else, contributes to feeding our mental activity through our conversations, the tasks we have to perform, the interactions we have with one another. Not to mention society, for it also influences our thoughts significantly, especially via the media.

- **Our flesh**

    Humans often feel torn between good and bad. Deep inside us, the good is encapsulated in our conscience, and yet, without understanding the exact reasons, we can be overtaken and defeated by the bad when a particular situation arises. We then get carried away by anger, jealousy, envy, the lack of forgiveness, or resentment. When someone doesn't have enough self-control, they can go as far as to say or do some things they later regret, once they calm down.

- **The enemy of our souls**

Some of our thoughts are whispered by the enemy of our souls. Just like he seduced Adam and Eve in the garden, the devil keeps doing so nowadays by whispering subtle thoughts to our soul. It is no accident that he is dubbed "the enemy of our souls", for his attacks are mainly concentrating at the level of our thoughts. Everyone's responsibility is to identify them, then accept or reject them. Hence the importance of the Bible, which sheds light on his strategies, and thus helps you to discern them. The enemy knows that if he manages to control your thoughts, he will also control your soul, and therefore your body. A lot of news items about some serious incidents (homicides, violence, torture) have been reported in recent years. Many times, the perpetrators were unable to explain the reasons for their atrocious acts, as if they had completely lost their mind for a moment.

- **God**

God talks to everyone, to children and adults, whether believers or non-believers. He may talk to them through dreams, visions, beliefs, intuitions, or thoughts, as written in the Book of Job:

> *For God may speak in one way, or in another, yet man* does not perceive it. *In a dream, in a vision of the night, when deep sleep falls on men, while they slumber on their beds.* (Job 33:14-15)

When it occurs, the non-believers are not always aware that God is speaking to them, but some do acknowledge that listening to their gut allowed them to escape some seriously critical situations, or to benefit from very advantageous conditions. The day when these people genuinely meet God and start journeying with Him, some memories of past events resurface, and suddenly they become deeply convinced that God intervened very precisely at that time. They realize with great emotion that God's eyes were already on them, while they didn't even know Him yet. Many testimonies point in this direction, some people even adding that if God hadn't kept them alive, they would have passed away. Back then, they thought it was just luck, but years later, they profoundly assume it was God saving them from great misfortune. Why them specifically, instead of someone else? This remains a mystery and demonstrates again that God's sovereignty prevails at any rate.

On November 28, 2016, the plane of the Brazilian soccer team of Chapecoense crashed, as they were flying to Medellin, Colombia, for the Copa Sudamericana finals. Out of the seventy-seven passengers, only six survived. Helio Hermito Neto, one of them, recalls that a few days before the flight, he had a horrible nightmare in which he could see himself on a plane, with heavy rain pouring outside. In his dream, the plane eventually crashed down but he survived. When he woke up, he was shocked: his dream was so vivid. The day of the trip, he just couldn't get the nightmare out of his head. Below is the narrative he shared in an interview given to the Players' Tribune[5]:

---

5. The Players' Tribune, interview of the 3 players who survived, Neto, Jackson Follma, Alan Ruschel, published on August 23, 2017: https://www.theplayerstribune.com/chapecoense-tomorrow-belongs-to-god/

> *On the day of the trip to the finals, I couldn't get the nightmare out of my mind. The dream was so vivid. It was hammering in my mind. So, I sent a message to my wife from the airplane. I told her to pray to God to protect me from that dream. I didn't want to believe that it was really going to happen. But I asked her to pray for me. And then I saw all the things from the dream really happening.... The plane shut off. The power went down completely. I was wide awake... Then the plane fell from the sky. It was beyond our comprehension as humans. I remember my last words in the plane. I was praying, praying, praying out loud. When I saw the airplane was definitely going to fall for real ... I said, "Jesus, Jesus, I read in the Bible that you made so many miracles. Please, please be merciful of us. Look after us. Help us. Help the pilot. Help us in this plane. Be merciful. Please, Jesus, help us."*

Helio Hermito Neto and two other players survived the crash. When it happened, Neto, his wife, and his two mates—also believers—were praying and imploring God's help. Why them? Only God knows. But one thing is sure: Neto, a believer, had had a dream warning him about the coming tragedy a few days prior to the crash. God's providential hand then rescued them.

- **Recognizing God's voice**

    Differentiating our thoughts from those coming from God is a pretty challenging task, for they all get mixed up. The moments of silence and reflection are becoming rarer and rarer due to our frantic pace of life that pushes us to live and act almost automatically, and besides, the occasions to enjoy some spare time to stop and listen to ourselves are limited. Immediately when we start the day, we tend to switch on our computer or our TV, check our phone, play some music, our attention swallowed up by all sorts of interests. Yet, to be aware that a thought doesn't come from us, we first need to know ourselves and/or the one transmitting it. Therefore, if we consider God the Source of Life, every positive and perfect thought inviting us to behave as such is very likely to originate from Him.

Summary:

- Real freedom is not so much about what we can do, but rather about what we are. It is only accessible to those who discover who they really are deep inside, before the social and societal factors began to mold their identity and, above all, those who strive to become so.

- Moses had to deconstruct his false perception of himself in order to break free and become the leader of an entire people.

- Thanks to neuroscience, we now know that when we transform the way we think, the change that occurs is not just mental, but also cerebral.

- In the end, the outer world is just the reflection of the inner universe of humankind, and the state of our modern societies is in fact the shadow of what's secretly happening in Man's heart.

Questions:

- Do you feel completely free? If not, explain why.

- Do you have any kind of addiction? The Apostle Paul wrote: *"People are slaves to whatever has mastered them."* (2 Peter 2:19). In order to answer as objectively as possible, one thing you can try is to take one or more days off the phone and social networks, or off anything else you are strongly attached to.

- Which certainties and reasonings appear to be obstacles in your life?

- With a view to receiving the revelation and finding out who you really are, which wounds do you need to heal, and which fortresses should you deconstruct?

Chapter 7 – I am...

Try it out and ask people around you: *"who are you?"*. You will be both surprised and amused at everyone's reactions, and at the expressions on their faces when in deep thought, looking for the right answer. Some people like to define themselves by their job: I'm a lawyer, I'm a teacher, I'm a taxi driver. The use of *"I am"* highlights that their self-image is mostly based on their occupation. One problem encountered by this category of people arises when they lose their job or when they become unable to work, for some reason: the sudden change of status gives them the impression that they no longer have any value and don't exist anymore. The reasons for this are very simple: in fact, their identity is somehow tied to what they do for a living. Other people tend to define themselves by their social status, the amount of money they have in their bank account, the cachet of their car, their lifestyle, or how many belongings they possess. They find satisfaction in achieving the personal goals they have initially established, such as being in a relationship, starting a family, setting up their own business, or fulfilling their dreams. These are not inherently bad, but they are perceived as the only symbols of success and happiness. The modern world likes to convey the general belief that it is actually what we own and accomplish that makes us happy. This message is constantly spread in the media, commercials, magazines, TV shows, and on the

Internet, every single day. Some TV shows have even specialized in storytelling reports showing ordinary people who achieved success thanks to their talent and work. They showcase their notoriety, number of fans, income generated, and lifestyle, as signs of success. **This approach leads a large number of people to believe that happiness ultimately consists in doing and owning, rather than merely being.** This popular belief is in fact so deeply anchored in society that those meeting all these criteria assume they have succeeded, while the rest feel they have wasted their life and missed out on it.

In 2007 the famed publicist Jacques Séguéla sparked outrage in the media after claiming: *"Everyone has a Rolex. If you don't have a Rolex by the time you reach 50, then you have clearly failed in your life"*. With these words, he was in fact attempting to defend former French President Nicolas Sarkozy, who was bombarded with criticism after being seen wearing a Rolex. Many blamed him for looking down upon the middle and lower classes, having a distorted vision of success in life. Wearing a Rolex isn't chocking in itself, especially considering the ex-president's earnings. But I found this anecdote interesting for two reasons. First, Jacques Séguéla sees possessing expensive belongings as a sign of success. Simply put, his perspective is all about **having** in order to **be**. The second reason is that the ones who accused him of being disdainful toward the middle and poorer classes actually shared the same views. So, why were they offended? Simply because the level of wealth set by the publicist as a pretended sign of success wasn't accessible to anyone, plus it was excluding a part of the population. Had he chosen something else like a car or a house, it would have sounded less shocking because a large amount of people can afford these, on credit... Society has somehow defined the standards of success and happiness by creating a sort of virtuous circle in which those who appropriate its principles and success values are included, whereas those who don't are left out. Thus, the actions and goods owned by a person ultimately determine who they are, according to this postulate.

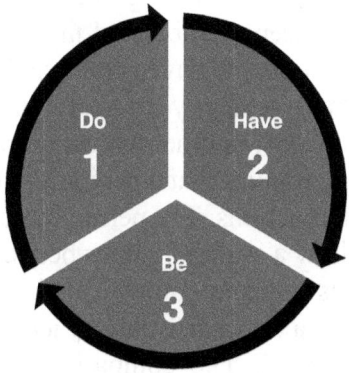

Most people endeavor to apply the principles and values preached by society in the hope of finding the much-heralded happiness. However, after a while, many realize they haven't reached the expected satisfaction. The most daring even decide to quit everything, and radically change their living environment, job, country, sometimes their partner, hoping to find the bliss they yearn for so badly. Over time and despite all their efforts, dissatisfaction starts haunting them again. Some give up and tell themselves: "That's how life is, after all!". Others still try to find the causes by turning to religion, by delving into philosophical readings, or by starting a self-introspection in order to understand. They don't really know how to express it, but deep inside themselves they feel a gap between what they're going through, what they are, and what they should be.

1 - "I AM what I do"

One day on arriving at Paris - Charles de Gaulle Airport, I saw a huge advertising board with **"I am what I do"** plastered on it. It was an ad for a top-selling brand's latest smartphone. This concept is so deeply embedded in our society's system of thought that most people have acknowledged and accepted it. Indeed, they have perfectly integrated the following fact: "they are what they do". In other words, *those who do nothing are nothing*, which implies that a person's value is likely to be determined by their actions. The pernicious effect of this popular belief is to draw a scale of values between individuals. It somehow compels them to compete with each other, which typically generates a lot of frustration, jealousy, insecurities, and self-esteem issues. The comparison is made at every level, whether physical, professional, intellectual, and many more. Moreover, it starts very early, with the school grades, rankings, contests of all kinds, and sports competitions. It goes on during adulthood, when some people compare their professional careers, salaries, social statuses, and belongings. Sadly, it generates envy to the point where those who are not strong enough, identity-wise, have the feeling that they would be happier if they were or acted like others.

If society's system of thought puts forward the fact that: **"I am what I do"**, the Bible, for its part, has a whole different point of view. I would like to introduce you to it through the story of the Apostle Paul, by showing you how this man was living an existence full of assumptions and beliefs until the day his path crossed that of Jesus. After this encounter, his deepest views were blown to pieces, for he discovered who he really was.

2 - The Apostle Paul's identity change

Before being known under his apostle name, Paul used to be baptized Saul. He grew up learning the Jewish religion with Gamaliel, a highly-reputed doctor and teacher of the law. Saul was a member of the Jewish party of the Pharisees, a very strict religious group. He used to persecute and jail the men and women claiming that Jesus was the Christ. One day he attended the death by stoning of Stephen, a young man stating that Jesus was the Messiah, and he approved the murderers' actions. Saul was convinced he was doing the right thing, for he was striving to protect and uphold the traditions of his fathers. The way he was looking at Jesus and his followers at the time was greatly influenced by his personal views, all coming from his family education (his father was a Pharisee too), religious beliefs, environment (Pharisee friends), and his excessive zeal for religion. Saul was then far from imagining how mistaken his assumption about Jesus was, because he was seeing Him through the prism of his religion. One day, as he was journeying to the city of Damascus, he suddenly found himself bathing in light, and a strong voice emerged: *"Saul, why are you persecuting me?"*. Saul fell to the ground and said: *"Who are you, Lord?"*. Then he heard: *"I am Jesus, whom you are persecuting"*. Saul replied: *"Lord, what do you want me to do?"*. The light was so intense that he went blind. The men traveling with him had to lead him by the hand into Damascus, where he stayed three days without eating or drinking anything. On the third day Jesus came to a disciple called Ananias, in a vision, and asked him to go find Saul and pray for his recovery of sight. Ananias, who had heard many reports about Saul, explained he knew all the harm he had done, but Jesus reassured him by revealing what He had destined Saul for. He said:

> *Go, for **this man is my chosen instrument** to take my name to Gentiles, kings, and Israelites. I will show him how much he must suffer for my name.* (Acts 9:15)

During his three days neither eating nor drinking, Saul had more than sufficient time to think. He realized how mistaken he was, and how what he was fiercely fighting against was in fact true. Immediately after Ananias prayed for him, Saul recovered his sight, and without losing time, he committed to serve God right away. Once again, this story portrays a person convinced of their beliefs, for they correspond to what they always learned and knew, but who finally realizes they were wrong. Let's imagine if someone met Saul at the time and inquired about his identity. He would respond right away: *"I'm a Pharisee!"* because it is the identity he gained from his family background and the religious environment he grew up in.

- **Paul's new identity**

The Apostle Paul received the revelation of his true identity the day he met Jesus. He realized he was *an instrument chosen by Jesus to proclaim His name before nations*. Yet, he was formerly convinced to be serving the cause of God before, but he did not suspect his motives to be wrong, for he was mistaken about his identity. He was driven by his own beliefs and reasonings. He needed this face-to-face encounter with Jesus to stop seeing the world and himself through his own eyes, but through God's eyes instead. When Ananias prays for him, a very interesting point is highlighted in the Bible: *"And immediately something like scales fell from his eyes, and he regained his sight."* (Acts 9:18). This sentence has to be understood in two ways: literally and spiritually.

The scales symbolize his physical but also spiritual blindness. When Ananias prayed for Paul, the Holy Spirit came and made His home in him, and the spiritual veil maintaining him in the dark was removed. His life changed radically. Henceforth, he was no longer only guided by his senses, emotions, and human thoughts, but by the Spirit of God. The trajectory of his life changed completely the day he was revealed who he was in the eyes of God.

The Apostle Paul is one of the most prolific authors of the Bible given he wrote, under the inspiration of the Holy Spirit, no less than thirteen books out of the twenty-seven of the New Testament. The introduction of each is more or less alike. Typically, the first two verses aim to introduce himself, mentioning whether other people are accompanying him, then Paul emphasizes the fact that his legitimacy doesn't come from men, but from God. Initially, the books written by Paul were letters addressed to churches, with the exception of four of them, written for his collaborators Timothy, Philemon, and Titus. When Paul addresses his friends, the tone is different, the presentation is less formal and far more personal. In his letter to Titus, the words chosen to introduce himself are so precise that it seems obvious he clearly knew who he was and what God had called him for. To me, that passage was like a revelation because by observing the way he introduces himself, the Holy Spirit showed me several keys which can be applied to everyone's identify. This enabled me to grasp what the identity according to God was, and thus comprehend mine. That's the reason why I'm willing to share these keys with you, for I believe they will help you discover your identity, too.

- **Paul's introduction**

As an excellent communicator, Paul manages to disclose his identity with just one verse. The Anglo-Saxons call this communication exercise a "pitch". A pitch is the ability to very briefly summarize a presentation, a story, a book, a CV. Some people master this discipline as well as the art of presenting all the key elements likely to grow the interlocutor's interest in a very short time. We shall not scrutinize the thirteen introductions but the one addressed to Titus, so you see how well the Apostle Paul knew who he was. He wrote:

> Paul, a **servant of God and an apostle** of Jesus Christ **to further the faith of God's elect and their knowledge of the truth that leads to godliness** (…) (Titus: 1:1)

Paul starts off by giving **his first name**. Behind this name lies his entire life story, together with what defines him as an individual.

- **His first name**

In Jewish culture, a name is rarely chosen at random, for it is meant to correspond to the character and personality of the individual bearing it. It is supposed to be an inspiration received by both parents. Saul changed his Hebrew name, meaning "asked for, inquired of God", to Paul. We ignore the reason for this, given no explanation is mentioned in the Bible, but we can presume he was intending to show reverence to the greatness of God, for Paul means "small and humble" in Latin. Moreover, at some point he wrote about himself: "**To**

me, though I am the very least of all the saints, this grace was given, to preach to the Gentiles the unsearchable riches of Christ (...)" (Ephesians 3:8)

Other Bible characters such as Abraham, the Apostle Peter, or Jacob[1] also changed their first names, but this time, we do know why. God changed Abram's name, meaning "high father", to Abraham, which means "father of many, father of a multitude", because it was more in line with his new identity: that of a father of a multitude of nations[2]. The same goes for the Apostle Peter. Similarly, Jesus changed Simon, his original name, to Cephas, which means Peter, explaining: "And I tell you, you are Peter, and on this rock I will build my church, and the gates of hell shall not prevail against it.[3]" Thus, Peter's new name was consistent with his new identity. He was not a simple fisherman anymore: from then on, he was a fisher of men, a pillar God would rely on to build His church.

Why does God rename some people in the Bible? The reasons are the following:

- Their identity and destiny are directly tied to their first name. By changing their names, not only does He reveal who they are, but He realigns them with the story He wrote for them. Their change of name also implied that the ones calling them thereafter would unknowingly proclaim the identity associated with the name. It may sound like a minor detail unless we know how powerful spoken words can be. The Bible supports this point through this verse: "Death and life are in the power of the tongue, and those who love it will eat its fruit." (Proverbs 18:21)

---

1. Jacob's name was changed to Israel (Genesis 32:28)
2. Genesis 17:5
3. Matthew 16:18

- Every person needs to **know who he or she** is in order to **become** that person. It is impossible as long as they ignore so. Knowing their true identity therefore generates profound changes which lead to transformation.

These examples illustrate that in God's mind, a name is much more than just a simple designation: it is meant to represent the story of the person bearing it.

- **His consecration**

Paul introduces himself as a **servant of God**. This being indicated right after his name underlines how important that information is to him, for it evidences that he willingly chose to dedicate his life to serving God. Besides, we saw earlier that Jesus had chosen him as an instrument to proclaim His name before nations, but he still had to accept. Paul's consent allowed God to assign him to a department where he would be able to serve Him.

- **His vocation and purpose**

God decides to make him an **apostle** of Jesus Christ. The word apostle originates from the Greek term *apostolos*, which means "a delegate, messenger, one sent forth with orders[4]". It was borrowed from the military parlance and usually refers to a military officer sent to a specific geographical area to establish a gamut of laws and rules accompanying the colonizing nation. The dissemination of the Gospel message was done

---

4. Definition of *"Apostolos"*, see: https://www.biblestudytools.com/lexicons/greek/nas/apostolos.html

through the Apostle Paul's teachings. That is why he wrote: "For the sake of this gospel I was appointed to be a **preacher**, an **apostle**, and a teacher of the Gentiles." (2 Timothy 1:11). The preacher[5] is the one who proclaims the Word of God.

Then, Paul discloses the **purpose** for which he was appointed apostle: *"to further the faith of God's elect and their knowledge of the truth that leads to godliness."* With this brief introduction, Paul explains that God destined him to be His messenger, with the mission of teaching the elect of God by revealing His principles and mysteries to them.

In short, Paul describes himself through four steps. First, he gives his **first name**, followed by his **profile**: servant of god, then comes his **vocation**, and lastly the **purpose of his mission**, as shown in the table below.

FIRST NAME (1)		
PROFILE (2)	VOCATION (3)	PURPOSE/MISSION (4)

By personalizing his presentation, here is what we get:

PAUL'S IDENTITY		
PROFILE Servant of God Field: ministry	VOCATION Apostle, Preacher	PURPOSE/MISSION To further the faith of the elect and their knowledge of the truth

---

5. Definition of preacher: "to call, to cry or proclaim as a herald, to announce good news", see: https://www.biblestudytools.com/dictionary/preacher-preaching/

Paul was a herald proclaiming the gospel of Christ. (John MacArthur Study Bible)

Paul had deliberately chosen to be a servant of God, it was in fact the prerequisites for God to be able to use him. As a servant of God, he had been destined by God to serve in the ministry. This service includes the following five ministries: evangelistic, teaching, pastoral, prophetic, and apostolic. God appointed him to the apostolic ministry, of which the mission was: *"to further the faith of the elect and their knowledge of the truth that leads to godliness."* Something interesting to point out is how his role and mission perfectly fitted him. Paul was a strong-willed and passionate man and every time he performed something, he was fully devoted (like when he was a Pharisee). His slightly extreme temper pushed him to commit awful acts when he was on the wrong side, however he later turned out to be a high-caliber asset when he was faced with the many challenges of his mission, and when it managed to persist without losing courage nor giving up. His religious background proved to be useful, too, when it came to debating with the religious leaders and trying to convince them. **Paul's character traits were in harmony with his true identity, yet he was misusing them when unknowingly walking in the wrong direction.** Just like the lion cub followed the old lion, Paul followed Jesus in embarking on the path destined for him. For this change to occur in him, he preliminarily had to rearrange his destination by changing his mindset. In adjusting his mind to God's mind and in allowing himself to be transformed through the renewal of his intelligence, Paul eventually became the man he was meant to be.

Let's look at the transformation that took place in him:

CHARACTER-ISTICS	FORMERLY KNOWN AS SAUL	MIND RENEWAL	LATER KNOWN AS PAUL
His genetic heritage	Genes inherited from his parents.		-
His culture	Roman citizen		-

His character traits	Stubbornness and zeal.		Integrity, passion, perseverance, love, heart for the lost.
His education and knowledge	He learned to make tents. He was raised in his fathers' religion.		His knowledge then comes from the revelations he received from Jesus Christ, enabling him to lay the foundations of the Church and Christianity. (see Galatians 1:11-12) His knowledge of the religious laws enables him to stand up to the religious leaders.
His system of thought	The instruction he received from his Father and Gamaliel influenced his beliefs as well as his way of seeing things, talking, and behaving.		The Holy Spirit deconstructed his former system of thought, and He transformed Paul by renewing his mind. His thoughts are henceforth guided and inspired by the Holy Spirit.
His mission	To destroy the church of Christ.		One of the greatest ambassadors of Christianity.

When you look at Paul as an inspiring model, you note that the concept of identity is different than the one conveyed by society. While the system of thought of society claims: "**I am what I do**", the Apostle Paul defines it in a completely dissimilar way. He says that being a servant of God makes him an apostle. In other words: "**I do what I am**", or: "**I am, therefore I do**". The difference can seem insignificant at first glance, but as soon as we get the meaning of both approaches, we see how poles apart they are. **While society puts forward the theory according to which what we do justifies what we are, the Holy Scriptures actually explain that what we are determines what we do.**

3 - "I do what I AM"

I would now like to introduce you to the life paths of Esther, Mark, and Carl[6]. These three people are believers and have deliberately chosen to put God first in their lives. After reading about their stories, you will better understand how knowing their identity guides their actions, not the other way around. Once you are able to clearly identify the elements that characterize someone, it gets impressive to see how their personality, mentality, skills, abilities—whether physical or intellectual—fully coincide with their life mission.

- **Esther: a passionate heart for the disadvantaged**

Esther grew up in an atheist family, with parents telling her that God didn't exist. During her childhood, she used to see herself in Africa in recurrent dreams, taking care of orphans and feeding the needy. She always wanted to help the most disadvantaged with all her heart, as if it was literally part of her. Once a teenager, she fulfills her childhood dream and travels to Senegal to volunteer for a humanitarian association to look after sick Talibé children[7]. Her experience there is like a revelation. She is so touched by everything she sees that she keeps going back every year.

---

6. The names have been changed to protect the privacy of the people involved.

7. A talibé is a boy from a poor family, who studies the Quran at a daara (West African equivalent of madrasa). This education is guided by a teacher known as a marabout but some of them, instead of teaching their talibés about the Quran, exploit them for labor, typically through forced begging on the streets. The nature of this exploitation exposes such talibés to disease, injury, death, physical abuse, and sexual abuse. See Wikipedia: https://en.wikipedia.org/wiki/Talibe

After a mission of several weeks in Senegal, she comes back deeply saddened, feeling totally helpless when faced with all the sufferings of the sick, abused, and left alone children. One night, as she is partying with a friend, she drinks some alcohol, probably a little too much, in order to numb her emotional pain. Under the relaxing effect of the booze, she starts speaking to God: "God, if you do exist, why are you letting these children suffer?" Then she goes on, yelling at that God she doesn't know. Witnessing the whole scene, her friend grabs a sheet of paper and writes down everything Esther is saying. The next day, after getting up, Esther reads what her friend wrote the night before. She's surprised by everything she happened to say.

One day a friend of Esther's invites her to church. At first, she is reluctant, but she eventually accepts, to please him. During the praise, while listening to a song, she suddenly feels overwhelmed by God, like carried off by a powerful current. She begins to shout: "Jesus! Jesus! Jesus!", although nobody really told her who He was. That day, she instantly receives the revelation that Jesus Christ is in fact God, and that He forgives all her sins. She progressively draws closer to Him, and finally discovers her true identity. He reveals it to her one day through the Holy Scriptures, when she comes across the following passage:

> *I, the Lord, have called you in righteousness; I will take hold of your hand. I will keep you and will make you to be a covenant for the people and a light for the Gentiles, to open eyes that are blind, to free captives from prison and to release from the dungeon those who sit in darkness.* (Isaiah 42:6-7)

A few months later she stumbles on the paper written by her friend in Senegal, and immediately realizes that what God is calling her to do corresponds to what she was actually blaming Him for, a few years earlier, when she was unware of His existence. She then understands that her childhood dreams were picturing what God had destined her for. She nevertheless needed to get close to Him to know her true identity. God was waiting for the right time to reveal Himself to her.

Esther spent a few years working for the Samu social in France, a municipal humanitarian emergency service, in order to help homeless people get off the streets, and she also worked for the Aide Sociale à l'Enfance, which translates as "social assistance to children", to take care of children subjected to violence of all kinds. In 2017 she goes back to Africa to help orphan children in Guinea, but that time she sees God at work through healings, miracles, and the revelation of His infinite love. Her helplessness of yesterday in front of those suffering children has been replaced by her seeing God's hand support her and act through her. In July 2018 Esther joins a missionary base founded in Senegal to help children get off the streets. The managers then offer her the same position as the one she had when working for the Samu social. At that point, she understands that all these years were in fact a sort of preparatory period.

ESTHER'S IDENTITY		
PROFILE Serving others Fields: Social work, Missionary*	**VOCATION** Missionary	**PURPOSE/MISSION** To restore the dignity of the weakest and the needy

*Unlike the humanitarian, missionary work also includes works related to the Christian faith such as charity and the preaching of the Gospel.

- **Mark: a heart willing to help others**

    Mark is a real-estate agent, and a believer. Although currently employed, he is considering going freelance shortly and launch his own real-estate franchise, with a view to tackling the problems associated with inadequate housing, an issue dear to his heart. The money he will make will also enable him to invest in associative and cultural projects to provide financial assistance to young entrepreneurs with innovative ideas. He wants to use his earnings for good causes aiming to help people. Mark's profile is interesting because unlike Esther, his job is not his primary vocation. Indeed, he is presently a real-estate agent, but his vocation is entrepreneurship. His current profession is an intermediary step preparing him to fully embark on his vocation. Besides, Mark had absolutely no idea about his vocation before becoming a real-estate agent. He initially wanted to be a policeman, like his father. His grand-father and uncle for their part used to work for the National Gendarmerie, namely one of the two national police forces in France. Not really knowing what to do, he was planning to pursue a similar career, by imitation. It is after starting his new activity, and by dint of meeting people struggling to find affordable housing due to their low earnings, that his desire to help them became increasingly clear. Mark's example shows that while some people are aware of their vocation very early, others find it later in life, during their studies, professional experiences, and with maturity setting in. Like for Esther, the vocation is the means given by God to Mark to express who He is, and to manifest what He placed in Mark when He created him. God takes care of the homeless and the ones in need of financial support through the love for these people He has deposited in Mark. Mark's profile is therefore the following:

MARK'S IDENTITY		
PROFILE Entrepreneur Fields: Real estate	**VOCATION** To set up and manage a real estate agency	**PURPOSE/MISSION** To provide financial and housing support

- **Carl: a wisdom that transforms people**

Carl was a pastor for a good twenty years and during his Ministry time, he was simultaneously studying law, which later allowed him to become a lawyer. He then passed an entrance examination to become a local magistrate and to address current affairs, in order to decongest the courts. He wrote about fifteen books and set up several companies. With his special profile and multiple skills, he often gets invited to speak at conferences worldwide, as a consultant and teacher. Added to this is his being a city councilor where he lives. Therefore, Carl's profile goes as follows:

CARL'S IDENTITY		
PROFILE Adviser Fields : Ministry, Entrepreneurship, Teaching, Counseling	**VOCATION** To enlighten people by sharing his wisdom	**PURPOSE/MISSION** To transform the civil society with ethical and values-driven businesses

Carl's profile is highly interesting because it evidences that we are not limited to just one field: we can definitely juggle occupations. The various positions held by Carl can seem totally disparate at first glance, but when you study them closely, you can detect they all have one thing in common: counseling. Carl was born to counsel and transmit his wisdom. His gift lies in his ability to gain knowledge to enrich his wisdom and pass it on to others, and in different fields. When you closely look at Carl's profile, you happen to note that the particularity of the lawyer, the judge, the consultant, the city councilor, the pastor, and the conference speaker resides in their ability to express themselves, and on top of that, to be listened to. Moreover, being an author is quite logically linked to his vocation, given as a lawyer he must be able to prepare pleadings, as a judge he is required to write verdicts, as a pastor he has to compile preachings, and as a conference speaker he needs to draft his teachings. As for his entrepreneur role, it is simply related to his various activities as a counselor and author.

You probably noticed that despite his wearing many hats, Carl's purpose remains more or less the same: *"to transform the civil society and the business world by bringing in new strategies, and ethics and values in line with his faith"*. Carl believes God is able to address the many challenges encountered by society, that is why he is heartily committed to teach this to people so that they discover their calling and transform their environment. It is the message he's carrying and intending to communicate thanks to the varying roles he's lucky to perform. It is something he transmits when invited to serve as a pastor, to teach the faithful how to apply the Bible principles that can change society. He carries the same message when he puts on his judge or lawyer attire and deals with cases which demand both his wisdom and empathy. This message also inspires his publications as well as the advice he happens to dispense as a consultant or city councilor.

- **Be a facet of God on Earth**

When you read the stories of Paul, Esther, Mark, and Carl attentively, your attention gets caught by two things. First, their personality: it was sort of tailor-made. Paul was a passionate man. This trait was rather a flaw when he was stuck in a role that wasn't his, but as soon as he found his real place in life, it growingly became an exceptional quality of his. Esther is sensitive. She's always had empathy and a genuine compassion for the disadvantaged. Mark loves giving. Yet, he did not always have the gift of liberality since he himself acknowledges having been stingy when he was young. Carl takes pleasure in sharing his knowledge. The behavior and actions of these four persons do not require any particular effort from them, simply because they do what they were created for.

Moreover, when you take note of the reasons that pushed them to take action, you see they were all driven by love. One of love's characteristics is to put the interests of others above our own. The satisfaction we gain comes from contributing to people's happiness. It is not for nothing that the Bible says: "*It is more blessed to give than to receive.*" (Acts 20:35)

Love is God's language. He uses this means to communicate and reveal Himself to men, by pouring out his unconditional love into the hearts of his sons and daughters so they in turn pass it on. This love is endless, for it is inexhaustible, as pointed out in the following verse: "(…) *God's love has been poured into our hearts through the Holy Spirit, who has been given to us.*" (Romans 5:5). The people touched by this love who also seek to understand its origin end up tracing it back to Him, because He is the source.

The person who receives the revelation of their true identity finds out that God loves them, and that He created them in His own image and likeness. Therefore, their actions are no longer performed in order **to exist**, but simply **to be**. Those succeeding in being the person imagined by the Creator then **evolve into** a depiction of Him on Earth, or at least a tiny facet of His infinite grandeur. To this end, it is essential to be born again beforehand in order to be restored to the starting position of Man before his fall, for it is the only way **to be**, by letting the Holy Spirit operate through the renewed spirit. Little by little, the spirit takes precedence over the soul (personality) and influences it so that it sees, thinks, acts, and talks as wished by God. They then become the person created by God.

Summary:

- Many people define themselves by their job, social status, and earnings. This approach fuels the general belief that happiness consists in doing and owning, rather than merely being.

- Society's system of thought likes to claim: **"I am what I do"**. For its part, the Bible submits a completely different point of view: **"I do what I am"**, or **"I am, therefore I do"**.

- A person's identity is far beyond what we think, for it enables to make God visible to the world. It is somehow one of God's facets for manifesting Himself on Earth.

Questions:

- Which approach did you adopt before reading this book? **"I am what I do"** or **"I do what I am"**?

- How did you define yourself before?

- Do you tend to compare yourself to others? If so, why?

- Do you feel you are the person you are meant to be? If not, why?

Chapter 8 – Who are you?

Do you think you are the person God has created? Or rather, are you the fruit of your era and of your culture? The previous chapters have enabled us to understand how much the perception we have of ourselves is infused with the environment we evolve in. Thus, on the one hand, there is the way we see ourselves in society, and the one assigned to us by God, on the other hand. It can sound hard to comprehend, especially for the non-believers, but having myself been faced with both perspectives, I can assure you that understanding this mystery can answer the numerous questions you may have. Many people feel they are like stuck and stagnating in life. While they examine further leads to understand the reasons for this, they don't imagine a single second that it actually originates from their not being the ones they are meant to be. The explanations for this are quite simple, though. The desires and dreams enshrined in these individuals, which are exactly what God would like them to fulfill, remain dormant until the day they find out who they truly are, because they directly depend on this.

Some people get close to it without even knowing God, thanks to the family, social, and cultural backgrounds they have benefited from, all of which favorably stimulated their personality to bloom. This helped them to find, forge, and learn to love themselves. It is something extremely important in our society marked by the dictate of fashion and success standards, which do not fail to encourage people to develop a growing lack of self-confidence and self-esteem. Others are not so fortunate and remain far from what God had initially planned for them. Lastly, there are the ones who, because they drew closer to God at some point, managed to know, if not rediscover themselves through this relationship. Today, they can confidently state: "I know who I am!".

1 - Your transformation process

- **Intellectual and emotional transformation**

When you are aware that God created you as a unique being, your ambition is no longer to look like one or another person, but to do everything possible to become your true self, instead. Of course, this change is not immediate, since there is a time gap between discovering and becoming so. This transformation process is a fascinating and disconcerting adventure at the same time, for it forces you to question quite a few elements you are attached to. Letting go of them will nevertheless be salutary, for even though you may not realize it on the spot, some of these elements keep you prisoner of your past, due to the influence they exert on your conscious, subconscious, as well as unconscious mind. One possible way to get rid of them is to carefully choose how you want to feed your mind (books, music, movies, talks, TV shows), in order to renew it with fresh ideas, more in line with the person you want to be.

- **Spiritual transformation**

Thankfully, you are not alone. The Holy Spirit supports you by operating some inner changes within yourself. His in-depth work is so profound that He can bring back to the surface some life events stored in your unconscious mind which are presently impacting your behavior. This can vary from one person to another, but He might soften up their temper or remove their pride, jealousy, anger, selfishness. He liberates from certain fears and limitations. He heals the internal wounds, ousts the evil thoughts, sets free from addictions. When this metamorphosis occurs, many feel they are sort of experiencing a "second birth", for they relearn to know themselves and even to love themselves, sometimes. The Holy Spirit also renews your mind to a level where your consciousness and emotions are in such perfect harmony that your spirit and your soul eventually become one. Those who successfully achieve this dimension encounter true freedom. The world around them ceases to hold sway over themselves, for their inner being is now strong enough to perform self-protection and overpower the external environment.

2 - Your identity

So, who are you?

I recommend you answer this question by drawing on the presentation template used for the Apostle Paul. That template is interesting because it forces you to choose the right words to describe your profile, your vocation, and your life purpose. Preliminarily, take a moment to pray so that the Holy Spirit inspires you, for your real identity doesn't come from your imagination, but from God's heart. Remember that the three are closely tied. From your profile stems your vocation, from your vocation arises your life purpose, and your life purpose depends on your profile. When you match them together, you get a clear portrayal of your past, your present, and your future.

These three questions will help you identify them:

Who?: Your profile

What?: Your vocation

How?: Your life purpose

Figure: Identity

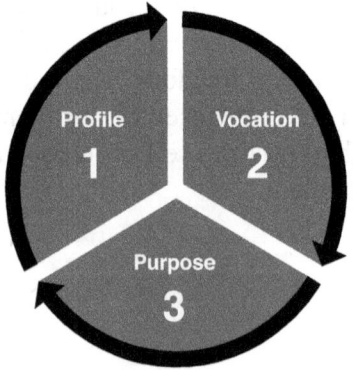

> *For we are his* **workmanship** *(poiema), created in Christ Jesus for good works, which God prepared beforehand so that we would walk in them.* (Ephesians 2:10)

The Bible translators chose the word "workmanship", considering it the closest translation to the original notion, but the Greek word used is *poiema*, which gave the words poetry and poem. *Poiema* suggests the idea that like poetry writing, God took His time to create you. God does nothing at random. He chose the color of your skin and eyes, the shape of your face and nose, He sketched your ears, He defined your hair type, and determined your voice tone. He gave you parents and grandparents and he transmitted some of their personality traits to you, such as sensitivity, empathy, gentleness, patience, creativity, enthusiasm, discipline, intelligence, wisdom, courage, or selflessness. Some people have a negative image of their parents because they were abandoned or not wanted. Maybe you are one of them? However, knowing that everything made by God is perfect, if life circumstances made your parents bad, loveless, and broken-inside persons, He still placed some good things for their own lives when He created them, thinking they would later be able to transmit those to you so you would become the person He imagined. Admittedly, some life courses are sometimes so tough that it is difficult for some people to accept them. Nevertheless, if you do feel affected, try to disregard their negative side in order to better discern the good things hidden deep inside them. You will then be surprised to notice that the way you look at them and yourself is different.

Among the numerous characteristics deposited in you by God, some make you genuinely unique, for they define who you are, in a very special way.

Questions:

- Which personality trait best describes you?
- Which personality tendency makes you stand out from the crowd? Which of your traits are usually pointed out by your loved ones?

- What touches you more than the rest, that you would like to see changed around you or in the world?

- **Your vocation**

The vocation is the means by which you will manifest your identity, by giving life to what dwells in you. Vocation can have several meanings, from religious to general. It comes from the Latin word *vocation*, from the verb *vocare*, which means to name or call. The Larousse dictionary defines vocation as Man's natural destination. This word has long been reserved for the religious spheres to refer to God's calling in one's life, also suggesting a notion of predestination. On a societal level, a vocation is perceived as a strong attraction toward an occupation or a certain lifestyle. Its discovery varies between individuals. Some will identify it at a young age, while for others it will happen much later in life. It is important to clearly distinguish between vocation and occupation, to avoid confusion. Unlike for a job, the primary motivations behind a vocation are neither the salary nor the social position, but the strong desire to give life to what's burning in our heart, with the deep conviction that in fulfilling it, we will accomplish what we exist for.

Questions:

- What is your job? Do you consider it your vocation? If not, do you know your vocation?
- What activity makes you feel fully alive?
- What would you like to do more than anything?

- Your purpose

Your purpose is the story you are meant to write on Earth. Most people acknowledge that a strong desire for something significant is burning deep inside them. This aspiration is legitimate, for it simply expresses the fact that we all exist for a purpose. When you get to talk with a creator, an inventor, or an engineer, and you ask them what inspired them to design such object, device, or machine, the first explanation they bring up is what it was created for, purpose-wise. Typically, they primarily identified a need, and invented an object in order to meet it. The product's characteristics are detailed in the user's guide coming with it, with its purpose first, how it works, its lifespan, not to mention the after-sales customer service, in case of malfunction. Of course, the lifespan and good condition depend on the user's ability to follow the manual and the recommendations of the creator or the manufacturer. The same goes for you: only the Creator can reveal why you exist and what your purpose is, the user's guide being the Bible. This encourages us to understand one thing: if there is a purpose, someone has to be responsible for it. Otherwise, how to explain that a purpose can be determined by itself? Similarly, how can one be sure to be using an object adequately, if ignoring its destination?

Questions:

- Do you know the purpose of your life? If so, what is it?

- Which mark would you like to leave on Earth?

- In what way would you like to make God visible?

When the timing feels right, try to fill in the following two tables:

YOUR FIRST NAME:		
YOUR PROFILE:	YOUR VOCATION:	YOUR PURPOSE/ MISSION :

	BEFORE	THOUGHT RENEWAL	AFTER
Genetic heritage			-
Your culture			-
Personality traits			
Your education and knowledge			
Your system of thought			
Your mission			

When you become aware of your inner identity, and when you eventually understand who you really are, then you can make every effort to embody your identity, at last, and therefore fulfill your destiny. You then realize that in your heart of hearts, you are holding all the assets that may meet the needs and expectations of the times you live in. Manifesting your real identity proves to be far more significant than what it seems. By becoming the person you should be, not only do you write the story as it was thought by God, but even more so. Your personal journey will then make its mark in the great History of Humanity, the one intended by the Creator for mankind.

I will thus conclude by asking you one last time: "Who are you?"

Summary:

- **Your profile:** Among the numerous characteristics deposited in you by God, some make you genuinely unique, for they define who you are in a very special way.

- **Your vocation** is the means by which you will manifest your identity, by giving life to what dwells in you.

- **Your purpose** is the story you are meant to write on Earth.

Conclusion

A deeply rooted tree can resist severe winds, storms, even some typhoons, unlike the shallow-rooted trees that can collapse anytime, at any gust of wind. Similarly, those who know who they are have enough control over their life to keep from being blown away and from risking to lose track of their earthly life purpose. Conversely, the ones ignoring it will be easily moldable and likely to accept what society says and expects from them. Today, the solutions to many of modern Man's ills lie in the understanding of humankind's identity, naturally speaking, but also and especially from a spiritual perspective. It is important that everyone comprehends this, for identity issues are and will be the challenges of the coming years. I hope this book has enabled you to discover your identity, in order to become the person God willingly made from the outset. Your life is in your hands, now it's up to you!

Special thanks

My deep gratitude to God the Father, God the Son, and God the Holy Spirit, the source of inspiration behind this project.

I also want to warmly thank Whitney Jean-Gilles, Thierry Grappotte, Guillaume, Eddy Kentsa, Melody Smit, Gaëlle Oustabachieff, and Marie-Anne Goury for the relevance of their proofreadings and observations.

Thank you to Marine Vlody, Kéna Kalala, Ruth Yapoga, Laetitia Benoit, Paskaline Seka, Hélène Hadassah, Sally Sangaré, and Max Nagels for their devotion; not to mention the technical expertise of Ulrich AK and Arowgrafiks.

Thank you to Marie Verpilleux for the translation of the book into English.

Table des matières

Introduction	11
FIRST PART **Identity according to Man**	15
Chapter 1 – Identity	17
Chapter 2 – The thought process	31
Chapter 3 – Personality	41
1 - Family	42
2 - Teaching	46
3 - Society	50
4 - The media	57
SECOND PART **Identity according to God**	63
Chapter 4 – Man according to God	65
Chapter 5 – Natural Man and spiritual Man	73
1 - Natural Man	76
2 - Spiritual Man	77
3 - Has society taken God's place?	83

Chapter 6 – Freedom 87

    1 - Moses: "Who am I?" 90

    2 - The renewal in humans 95

    3 - The various sources that feed the thoughts 106

Chapter 7 – I am… 113

    1 - "I AM what I do" 116

    2 - The Apostle Paul's identity change 117

    3 - "I do what I AM" 126

Chapter 8 – Who are you? 135

    1 - Your transformation process 136

    2 - Your identity 137

Conclusion 145

Special thanks 147

www.ingramcontent.com/pod-product-compliance
Lightning Source LLC
Chambersburg PA
CBHW071119090426
42736CB00012B/1959